Some Letters I Never Sent
(And one or two I did)

Some Letters I Never Sent

(And one or two I did)

MAX STAFFORD-CLARK

The Book Guild Ltd

First published in Great Britain in 2021 by
The Book Guild Ltd
9 Priory Business Park
Wistow Road, Kibworth
Leicestershire, LE8 0RX
Freephone: 0800 999 2982
www.bookguild.co.uk
Email: info@bookguild.co.uk
Twitter: @bookguild

Typeset in 11pt Minion Pro

Printed and bound in the UK by TJ Books LTD, Padstow, Cornwall

ISBN 978 1913913 748

British Library Cataloguing in Publication Data.
A catalogue record for this book is available from the British Library.

CONTENTS

FOREWORD BY
DANNY BOYLE

A good jockey doesn't need orders
and a bad jockey couldn't carry them out anyway;
so it's best not to give them any.

Lester Piggot.

Much the same might be said of actors and directors.

So what do directors do? Well, the good ones create a hinterland for the actor to step from and into the climate of the writing. And in the case of new writing - Max's speciality - the great ones promote an ecosystem of bravery and exploration: revolution through explanation and understanding rather than reliance on visual flair or theatrics.

No one comes close to Max in this regard.

His particular signature is a rigorous analysis of precisely why an actor is saying a line in both a personal and political sense. Max insists on an almost brutal examination of everything that passes before him. Crucially though, as he now acknowledges, this is everything except his own behaviour. It's salutary for all of us that his own use of language should be so offensive and triggered such consequences for him when as a professional he held writers and actors to pitiless account for their own relationship with language.

A second signature is his search for, and subsequent reverence for the underdog. Though you can sense his class and his advantage in life throughout these pieces, he uses those privileges to find, and triumph, the voice of the vulnerable wherever he can.

The marginalised most championed by Max and most important to his work was not class based - the blighted estate, working-class drama he portrayed so vividly - but women and their stories. And the colossus that bestrides his era is not one of the Edwards or the Davids or the Howards but Caryl Churchill. If you want to trace theatre's equivalent of Wonder Woman's blazing lasso you will find Caryl amongst its mercurial originators. In real world terms it's clear now that her theatrical revolution is more significant than John Osborne's ever was.

Max was instrumental in this revolution's scaffolding, the platform-building for female writers long before it was fashionable or urgent. He was also simultaneously, as he now admits, abusing language and his position of power in his relationships with some women. With this revelation his reputation is now inexorably tarnished.

To paraphrase Katherine Mansfield : These are not letters but my arms around you for a brief moment. Reaching for forgiveness, explanation, pity, redemption, Max has never really invited arms around himself until now and yet his ferocious, indignant attempt to rebuild his health and his reputation is almost intimidating, rebuffing sympathy even as he seeks it. As someone who remains deeply indebted to his lonely belief in my own prospects as a young trainee director I read these eloquent and witty essays with great sadness that his reputation has been shattered by the very freedoms and powers he encouraged. There's an almost unbelievable irony running throughout, humming like an electrified wire, that Max was both architect and villain in a world that turned upside down on him.

Danny Boyle

INTRODUCTION FROM
MICHAEL BILLINGTON

Dear Max,

Since your book consists entirely of letters, I thought I would send you my own epistle rather than write the formal introduction that you politely requested. As you point out, our careers have overlapped: I wrote my first review for *The Times* in May 1965 and your first professional production was at the Traverse, Edinburgh, in August of that year. In the half-century or more since, I have seen the bulk of your work with Joint Stock, the Royal Court and Out of Joint. And, although we have never been close – what critic and director ever are? – I have enjoyed our periodic professional encounters. So I approached your book with great interest.

The first thing to say is that it shows your deep regard for writers and actors and goes a long way to explaining your directorial methods. On the subject of dramatists, I never fully shared your admiration for Andrea Dunbar but you make a persuasive case for her. I am with you totally, however, on Caryl Churchill who, as you say, has changed the theatrical landscape. One of the first features I wrote on joining *The Guardian* in 1971 was a lament for the dearth of women dramatists. Shortly after, Churchill's *Owners* appeared at the Theatre Upstairs and since then she has never ceased to be a source of rich provocative experiment. As your Royal Court colleague James Macdonald once said, 'Caryl is always ahead of the game.' You also rightly point to the way she embraced the idea of creative workshops, verbatim texts and collective research on plays such as *Light Shining in Buckinghamshire*, *Serious Money* and *Cloud Nine*. It is true to say that if we now have a wealth of women dramatists, it is because Caryl Churchill, for all her personal reticence, has acted as a role-model and an inspiration.

You also say in your book that it is important to treat actors as your allies, and your imagined letters to Donal McCann, Gary Oldman, Rachel Roberts and Montgomery Clift (and I had no clue as to your connection to him) show your respect for their profession. Not only that. I was struck by the practical advice you give to a young actor about to play Harmon in a drama-school production of Sophocles's *Antigone*. I was especially impressed by your reminder that 'punctuation is a direction the writer bequeaths to the actor'. I only wish that advice were universally heeded. It is also a good example of the way practised professionals can pass on their experience to the next generation. By chance I am currently reading another book of theatrical letters: those between Bernard Shaw and Ellen Terry. At one point Shaw, writing in regards to Ellen's daughter, contrasts pianists who play scales for several hours a day before appearing in public with actors who lack muscle in the enunciation of words. As Shaw says, the actor should be able 'to drive a nail up to the head with one touch of a consonant'. It may seem odd to link you to Shaw but you both have the capacity to offer wise counsel to the young.

I was naturally intrigued by your letters to directors such as Bill Gaskill, Danny Boyle and Rufus Norris. It is often said that directors never know what their colleagues do in the rehearsal room. Certainly critics can only guess as to where credit truly belongs. But you state an important general truth in your letters: that the job of the director is 'to fulfil the writer's vision'. That lies at the core of your own work and that of a whole generation of Royal Court directors going back to George Devine, John Dexter, Anthony Page, Peter Gill and, of course, Gaskill. It is worth restating today at a time when directors are more often judged by the originality of their concepts than their fidelity to the writer, whether dead or alive. When I put this recently to a young director, he said there was an economic explanation: since it is difficult for a director to make a living in the British theatre, the temptation is to seek work on the European continent where a different ethos applies. I am all for close contact with Europe but, in this case, I find myself cleaving to the Royal Court idea of a director as a sensitive interpreter rather than an independently creative artist.

Your book, in short, is full of wise saws and modern instances; you also give a clear account of your own directorial method of 'actioning' which is when 'we describe the intention of a line with a transitive verb'. Ultimately derived from Stanislavski, this has had a big influence on British theatre: only recently I met a drama student who used the word 'actioning' as if it were now part of common currency.

But I have so far avoided the elephant in the room

which is your own current position in, or more strictly outside, British theatre. You address the subject in your two opening letters. You remind us how you were summarily dropped by Out of Joint after you were found to have made inappropriate remarks to a female colleague and how this was followed by other allegations of offensive behaviour. I should say straight away that I was shocked and dismayed when I read the reports and that I unequivocally support the move by women – and men too – to be treated with dignity, courtesy and consideration in the workplace.

Your letters, however, put your side of the story. You explain that a serious stroke had left you 'emotionally labile' and not always aware of the words that were coming out of your mouth. You go on to apologise to everyone you offended, to admit that 'I was in a position of power and did not always exercise it responsibly' and to say that you have suffered for your sins by being unable to work for three years. My own feeling is that it is time for forgiveness. Your family, notably your amazing wife, Stella, and your daughter, Kitty, have stood loyally by you during these difficult years. You have faced the facts about your faults. I only hope that truth can be followed by reconciliation.

Yours,
Michael

A CONTEXT

Dear Reader,

Each of us must take responsibility for our failings and I take responsibility for mine. In September 2017 a female colleague at Out of Joint wrote to the board alleging that I had engaged in 'inappropriate conversation' and had 'made comments of a sexual nature'. The complaint was taken seriously and following an investigation led by a member of the board I was asked to step down from the company.

At the time I was three days into rehearsal of *Rita Sue and Bob Too*, by Andrea Dunbar, which was a co-production with the Royal Court and the Bolton Octagon. I was to step down from the production immediately and leave it in the hands of my co-director and successor, Kate Wasserberg. I was forbidden to attend further rehearsals or to meet the cast to explain the situation. I could attend the first performance in Bolton only if I was accompanied by a member of the board, and under no circumstances was I permitted to speak to any of the cast or crew. With such conditions I saw little point in making the journey.

A month later the young woman who had made the original complaint went to *The Guardian* with the story. *The Guardian* journalist then conducted a trawl, phoning a number of high-profile actresses I had worked with and inviting them to comment on my behaviour. I know this because three of them phoned me to ask what was going on. I imagine the journalist must have phoned a dozen more. One complained about my behaviour towards her during a production at Stratford in the early '90s, and *The Guardian* duly ran a piece on the front page.

I was devastated by the collapse of my world and the shame that I had brought to my family. Further humiliation lay ahead: in October I was phoned by a student in her final year at drama school. She was to appear in a one-woman play on the Edinburgh Fringe and asked if I would help her work on it. My wife, Stella, took the trouble to explain the situation to her but she was unperturbed. There was no question of payment and indeed I was happy to pay for rehearsal space at the Islington Arts Factory. She took direction easily and I enjoyed working with her in the limited time we had together. She and the writer had secured space in Edinburgh in what appeared to be an old potting shed adjacent to a garden centre. My professional career had started 54 years earlier in Edinburgh, in Jim Haynes's tiny Paperback Bookshop in Charles Street. I took a grim satisfaction in the thought that it could well end in a potting shed only half a mile away. But it was not to be. After Christmas the author phoned to say that he thought my presence would create a distraction that could take the focus away from his play. I pointed out that on the highly competitive fringe, publicity of any kind was like water in the desert and that my presence might secure a modicum of critical coverage. I think we both had a point, but he disagreed and for the second time in six months I was fired – this time from a job I was doing for free.

There followed a bleak period of indulgent self-pity, succeeded by an extended one of self-examination. Throughout my working life I've been provocative, uninhibited, at times confrontational. I learned not to be deterred by criticism, but in doing so I became disrespectful of any contrary opinion. I took my work seriously for sure, but rarely myself and almost never the concerns of others. I said what I pleased and often exceeded the norms of office banter with members of the opposite sex. It's no excuse to say that it was a different time, or that others were doing the same, or that no one seemed to mind. I was in a position of power and did not always exercise it with responsibility.

But now I was forced to face my past. It's not been easy. I pulled open the closet and found few rattling skeletons. In fact, when I looked back on my life it was not things I had done but things I had not done that caused me shame: the broken promises, the vows evaded, the commitments discarded were strewn across the years like a trail of broken glass leading to a traffic accident. Perhaps it was little surprise to anyone but myself that I had landed in this situation.

I can only say that I deeply regret any behaviour of mine that has caused hurt or offence, and sincerely apologise to any who have been on the receiving end. If it is any consolation, the punishment has been duly severe. Theatre has been my life and its abrupt removal has been hard to bear. When I had a stroke in 2006 I woke up in the Whittington Hospital unable to move. From my hospital bed I planned Out of Joint's programme for the next two years, including a complex Anglo-Australian production of *The Convicts' Opera*. The support of my colleagues and the prospect of returning to work helped immeasurably in my recovery.

The grounds for my demise have been particularly hard to come to terms with, as I have been a champion of women's writing throughout my career – a list that includes Caryl Churchill, Timberlake Wertenbaker, Sue Townsend and Andrea Dunbar. In 1979, when I arrived at the Royal Court, 8% of the theatre's output since *Look Back in Anger* in 1956 had been authored by women. Over the 14 years I was there this rose to 38%, and in my 23 years at Out of Joint it was 48%. Almost my final act at Out of Joint was to programme *Close Quarters*, by Kate Bowen, and the revival of *Rita, Sue and Bob Too*, by Andrea Dunbar. This brought the overall output up to 50% exactly. None of this was as a result of positive discrimination. I was simply pursuing talent, but nonetheless I am very proud of the results.

For the past three years I have done little but read voraciously. However, recently I worked with some new and some valued and familiar colleagues on *A Critical Matter*, by Gareth Armstrong, an outstanding new play focusing on the life of the drama critic James Agate. This culminated in a reading for an invited audience. The work was enormously pleasurable, the reading warmly received and we are now in the early stages of planning a new company.

I recall meeting Sir Peter Hall in the car park one

morning at the RSC in Stratford in the early '90s. He had left the National two years earlier and I had just left the Royal Court. 'Are you going to do it again?' he enquired, and then added, 'I think I can do it just one more time.' He subsequently started the Peter Hall Company and I, with Sonia Friedman, started Out of Joint. Like Sir Peter Hall, I think I can do it one more time. I hope I'm right.

Best wishes,
Max Stafford-Clark

This letter and the one that follows are the two letters in this book that I did send. I realise that the advantage of so doing is that it considerably increases the likelihood of a response.

Nick Hern is a London-based independent specialist publisher of plays, theatre books and screenplays. He founded Nick Hern Books in 1988. Thirty years ago I approached him with the idea of combining the play text with the programme information. This made the text immediately available and guaranteed a not-insubstantial extra income for the playwright. This practice has since been widely adopted.

April 25, 2020

Dear Nick,

It is now nearly three months since your email of January 27, 2020, explaining in detail why you are unable to publish *Some Letters I Never Sent*. I am determined to reply, not with any hope of persuading you to change your opinion, but for my own peace of mind. Every so often I have written a page or two, only to discard it the next day.

As Dr Johnson wrote of *Paradise Lost*: 'A volume that once put down is very hard to pick up again.' I feel very much the same with my pen; it is very hard to summon the will to write. But I will try, starting with some of your literary criticisms, which, as I had anticipated, were thoughtful and pertinent.

You call the whole collection a 'hodge-podge'. I, rather more politely, term it 'a hybrid'. Perhaps we could agree on 'a miscellany'. It had always been my intention to mix a range of opinion with both autobiography and reminiscence. So no wonder the letters appear like 'chapters from different books'. That was always the plan. Specifically you describe the letter to the Ancestors as akin to 'random photographs in a family album'. Well, yes... that too was part of the intention. You use the definition dismissively, but surely the interest of any album depends on the quality and range of the photographs. I rate my godfather Guthrie Moir's poem to Lieutenant Taramoto as one of the most revealing and distressing war poems I have ever read, and I would love it to be known more widely. I also find my uncle Ian Stewart's first-hand account of the retreat and evacuation of Crete almost equally moving. And my father David's story of a horrific mid-air collision is brutally shocking and candid.

All these men – boys, really – were thrown into the war after rushed initial training to fight against a professional army that had been preparing for war for the previous ten years. It changed their lives forever. However, other readers (Gareth Armstrong, Danny Boyle, Roger Michell and my brother Nigel) have also found the letter unanchored, and I see that I have avoided writing about my own relationship with, and the influence of, these men. I surmise that the link is to be found in the veteran bomber captain's statement that, 'We all shared a responsibility to create some kind of hopeful future for the world; something good, or at least better.' This is the philosophy I inherited and, without wanting to sound pretentious, I believe it has characterised the best of the work I have commissioned or chosen to direct: the conviction and expectation that we can learn from history and point optimistically to a more equable and more equal way of living.

You urge the necessity for an underlying purpose or plan to link the letters together. I agree this is an essential requirement, but it is ironic that you yourself unwittingly defined the purpose for me. When you visited me in, I think, April or May 2018, you told me with great candour that your young staff regarded me as a 'kind of devil'. In your more recent email, nearly two years later, you write that you abhor the fact that I am a 'pariah' – there doesn't appear to have been much progress up the evolutionary ladder in the intervening time. In fact I think that being a devil is marginally preferable to being a pariah. So the purpose of the letters could be seen as an application to rejoin the human race – an unsuccessful application in your view, but I think I believe that with the combination of opinion and reminiscence I would reveal myself and would perhaps be seen more three-dimensionally once more. This purpose is still clearly obscure. But nevertheless, if the opportunity arises, I would be grateful if you could remind your young staff that in a Christian society repentance is followed by forgiveness.

Your email imagines I may be angry. Well, yes, I am

angry, and frustrated – mainly with myself for my stupidity and unthinking carelessness. But I am also frustrated that the hearing outlined by Out of Joint never took place and that I have had no opportunity to challenge any of the allegations. Some were just, and for these I have been punished. I am truly sorry for my unpleasant behaviour. But some allegations were silly. For example, it was alleged that I had lured a female colleague into my office to read a lewd and pornographic scene from a play. The play was in fact *Cloud 9*, by Caryl Churchill, and the colleague was the education manager, who had never seen or read it. I had been asked to conduct a workshop at a school which had chosen the play for a school production. You will recall that one of the storylines concerns an explicit relationship between a nine-year-old boy (played by Julie Covington in the original production) and an eminent Victorian explorer in early middle age. I was endeavouring to find a suitable scene to work on with a mixed group of 16- and 17-year-olds, and also to alert the education manager to the nature of the material.

As your email succinctly and correctly points out, I stand condemned either for ignoring the situation I am in or for attempting a defence which could be seen, in your words, as 'special pleading, whingeing or unjustified self-justification'.

Since this letter is not intended for publication (not at the moment at any rate) I feel able to recount a pertinent medical history. Following the stroke (or series of strokes) I had in 2006 there were a number of side effects I sustained as a result of the brain damage that had occurred. Most were immediately apparent to me, and I have been able to employ strategies to cope with them. For example, my left peripheral vision is severely impaired by irreversible damage to the blood vessels leading to the eyes, and when reading I have had to train myself to look fully to the left of the page. This I have done, and over the past three years I have read more extensively than in any other period of my life.

Another deficit is that I am 'emotionally labile'. This means that the damage to the frontal lobe of the brain makes the sufferer 'emotionally incontinent'. It can take the form of uncontrollable temper, inappropriate and prolonged laughter, or a proneness to tears. With me it is the latter. Incidents which would move anybody have me weeping uncontrollably. For example, a few years ago a group of Chilean miners were trapped underground for over a week. The news item featuring their rescue was undeniably moving, but for the next 20 minutes I was unable to stop myself crying. This weakness embarrasses my daughter, Kitty, particularly and, again, I have learned to control the impulse by thinking of tax returns or summer holidays or anything to divert the inclination.

There is a further side effect, of which I was completely unaware. On December 26, 2017, I fell heavily, on the upstairs landing of my flat, breaking my pelvis and fracturing my hip. These injuries necessitated lying on my back for 12 weeks while the bones reknitted. I returned home after hospitalisation in February but fell once more in March. On this occasion I misjudged the distance between the toilet pedestal and the hot rail and fell on the bathroom floor. Miraculously, I escaped serious injury, but I realised I was becoming dangerously accident-prone and concluded that I probably needed help.

After my stroke in 2006 I had spent two months recuperating in the National Hospital for Neurology and Neurosurgery in Queen's Square, and I now arranged a series of appointments with its senior neurologist, Professor Nick Fox, in his outpatients clinic. Because Professor Fox only sees NHS patients there is a six-month waiting list and my four appointments were spread over 18 months from May 2018.

I spent one day undertaking verbal, numerical and memory tests. On another visit I had had electrodes glued to my scalp, feeding a small computer carried in a pouch around my waist. I had to keep the electrodes on for 24 hours, but they showed conclusively that I was not prone to epileptic fits. There were many further scans, tests and X-rays. It was October 2019 before I received Professor Fox's report and assessment. At our final session Professor Fox told me I had scored 84 on the verbal tests, which was 'significantly above the average'. One point higher would have put me in the Einstein category! So part of my brain was functioning as well as ever. I was less impressive on the visual tests, and Professor Fox continued: 'The damage to the frontal lobe has caused a certain social blunting', as well as 'erosion to various inhibition centres'. He explained that the frontal lobe is the control centre of the brain. It monitors and controls decision-making. For example, it will say, 'Don't cross the road – you may have a green man but that car is approaching too fast and it's raining.'

Professor Fox emphasised that these findings were in line with what he had anticipated and were well-documented results of stroke.

After the final assessment I understood that my decision-making, both socially and spatially, had been out of my control for some time. For example, at an Out of Joint board meeting, a discussion had been prompted by the Arts Council on the issue of finding a successor. The board debated for some time whether or not they should advertise the post or invite particular applications. I finally said, 'Do both. Advertise and invite applications. And then the Arts Council and you can both fuck off.' Understandably this crass and clumsy intervention caused considerable consternation, particularly upsetting one board member who had been a constant and generous supporter of the company for many years. I apologised immediately and copiously.

On another occasion I got into trouble with Lloyd's Bank. One Sunday afternoon I attempted to transfer a small sum from my current account into the savings account. It was a frustrating telephone banking experience: twice I was cut off and once I keyed in an incorrect digit. Having finally completed the transaction, the young woman adviser asked if she could be of any further help. I had begun to reply when I was abruptly transferred to an older man who questioned me in detail about the conversation I'd just had. After a few minutes I asked what it was that he wanted to know. He told me that I had requested the young woman adviser to help me place a bomb in Lloyds headquarters! I had no recollection of this, though I clearly remembered my frustration. It took me a further 10 minutes to persuade the Lloyd's security officer (for this is who he was) that I was simply a dotty old codger and not a jihadist or a revolutionary.

I am certainly not claiming that every provocative or irresponsible remark I made between 2006 and 2017 was caused by the injuries I had suffered. But I am clear that my prevalent proclivity towards provocation was at times exacerbated and uncontrolled. With Professor Fox we discussed various helpful strategies to ensure I was more guarded and considerate in social situations. Professor Fox's final remark to me was: 'When you come to a decision and you think one thing and Stella thinks another, you should be aware that she is probably right and you are likely to be wrong.' Stella and Kitty remind me of this regularly. Provocation is a legitimate requirement for a director of new work; without it I would probably not have undertaken *A Thought in Three Parts*, *Shopping and Fucking*, *Rita, Sue and Bob Too*, or *Etta Jenks*. But, like my other deficits, awareness of it has enabled me to prevent any further inappropriate or offensive responses.

Well, that's enough 'unjustified self-justification and whingeing' for the moment, and I apologise for the length of this letter. You must have received many letters from disgruntled and rejected authors saying, in effect, 'Well, you may not have liked it, but I think it's rather good.'

Finally, thank you for the time and trouble you took with your lengthy email. I hope that your email and this response will not signal the conclusion of a friendship and business relationship which has given us both much pleasure over thirty years.

Best wishes, as ever,

Max

PS I am glad you feel that the letters to members of the profession work best, but it was to Andrea Dunbar, not Adrian Dunbar, that I wrote.

Michael Billington was *The Guardian*'s theatre critic for nearly 50 years. He is also a film critic and has written several biographies of well-known playwrights. Michael has contributed to *The New York Times* and television and radio broadcasts, presenting BBC Radio 4's *Kaleidoscope* and *Critics' Forum* arts programme. He was appointed an Officer of the Order of the British Empire (OBE) in the 2013 New Year's Honours for services to the theatre.

November 12, 2019

Dear Michael Billington,

I am sorry to hear that you are stepping down as leading theatre critic of *The Guardian*. Your contribution has been mighty. Our careers have run in parallel for nearly 50 years and during that time I have always searched first for your response. When it has been favourable I have been delighted, and when on the occasions (few, I'm glad to say) that I had a thumbs-down I have been mortified.

Our first meeting was during rehearsals of my first-ever production at the Royal Court: *Magnificence* by Howard Brenton. You were writing an editorial piece about Howard, I think, when you were invited to a rehearsal in the spring of 1973 – early days for both of us. It had been raining heavily and you were soaked. I want to write that you had to take off your trousers to have them dried and you watched the rehearsal in your underpants, but I may be making this up!

I think what I admire most is your undimmed appetite for and reckless optimism about the theatre. I remember observing you at one Edinburgh Festival tucking into a solid evening meal, possibly at Henderson's, near the Assembly Rooms, before marching away tirelessly on your evening beat once more.

I use the word 'appetite' advisedly. Over the past few years I have been to the theatre between 25 and 35 times a year. In the ten months so far of 2019 I have been on 18 occasions. Three were excellent evenings. One was the first revival of *The Permanent Way*; another was an adaptation by Stella, *The Omission of The Family Coleman*, in Bath; and the third was David Edgar's *Trying It On*. Two more were three-star evenings, two were unspeakable tosh and the remaining 11 induced various shades of disappointment. So why do I keep going to the theatre? Partly habit, partly curiosity and partly because when it is good there is no more thrilling a public event. But the ratio of dismay to elation is alarmingly high, and you must have had many a dismal evening in your 50 years in post, trying to restrain intemperance and abuse. I understand the attractions of evenings at home.

Sex and violence are, of course, the great stumbling blocks over which historically critics have regularly fallen. Drama critics should sleep with a copy of Clement Scott's review of Ibsen's *Ghosts* under their pillows to guard against tendencies towards abuse. Of *Ghosts* he wrote: 'An open sewer, a loathsome sore unbandaged.' Of course you have not been immune from the occasional stumble. You did penance for some months after you had over-hastily dismissed Sarah Kane's *Blasted*, and, like many of us, I don't think you realised the impact and enduring importance of Andrea Dunbar's work. As for *Shopping and Fucking* – probably the most successful play I have ever been involved with in terms of bums on seats – you thought little would linger afterwards beyond 'the vile smell of microwaved food'.

But I shall truly miss your weakness for extravagant puns. Anyone who endeavoured a production at the RSC that followed one by Terry Hands was quickly made aware that the lighting budget for the whole season was exhausted. So I cherished your review of Terry's opening production at Teatr Clwyd, when you commented: 'Many lights makes Hands work.'

Bravo.

Very best wishes for the future,

As ever, with great respect and admiration,

Max

Michael Billington wrote back, and here is a short extract from his letter:

…And you did indeed invite me to watch a rehearsal of *Magnificence*. I've looked up in *One Night Stands* what I wrote at the time: 'Arrive at Court in torrential downpour. Worried that I'll be sitting there all day in quietly steaming trousers. But if I take them off on arrival, will my gesture be misinterpreted?' Needless to say, I stayed fully clothed.

Dr D Bhatt, Clinical Associate Professor at the Department of Psychiatry, NYU Grossman School of Medicine and Director of the Psychiatry Residency Training Program.

July 13, 2020

Dear D,

I am relieved and delighted that you have now finished your tour of duty on the Covid-19 wards and returned to your psychiatric practice. When we talked in the middle of March you told me that on the Covid wards you had caught a bout of the virus yourself but that your symptoms had been relatively mild and that you had recovered within two weeks. But when we talked last night I realised that you had been extremely economical with the truth and that your illness had been far more serious than you had revealed.

We first met in 2007, when I was in New York directing JT Rogers' *The Overwhelming* at the Roundabout Theatre. Stella and I were staying at the Algonquin, where I had the first of several episodes of TGA (transient global amnesia). These are often rather misleadingly called 'mini-strokes', although the symptoms are more akin to an immediate onset of Alzheimer's, involving almost complete short-term memory loss. The one reassuring fact I was told by the medical team at the Presbyterian Hospital in New York – which was confirmed by the doctors I saw at the Whittington Hospital when I returned to London – was that these inexplicable episodes are extremely rare and most unlikely to recur. But no! I had three similar episodes in London in the course of two months in 2010, one in 2014 and absolutely none at all since then. No doctor, psychiatrist or neurologist has been able to explain why these brain blips happen or why they have so suddenly stopped. During my first episode in London an ambulance took me to the Royal London Hospital, and after a lengthy examination a young registrar pronounced: 'You appear to be having an episode of confusion.' I suppressed my inclination to respond, 'Well, I could have told you that.' It would have been unkind, and her analysis is the nearest to an explanation I have ever been given.

It was the Wednesday morning of the second week of rehearsal in New York, at about 6am or so. It's impossible to be accurate about this, because in a way I wasn't really there – I was stuck in a weird memory loop and couldn't find my way out. I woke up wanting to go to the loo and realised that I didn't know where the hell I was. I called out to Stella, who turned on the light. I was further alarmed to realise I didn't recognise the room. Apparently I repeated the same questions over and over again: 'Where am I? What is this? Why am I here?' I was not in search of answers as to the nature of existence. This was real confusion and chaos. What on earth was going on? When I attempted to get up and go to the loo, Stella rushed to my side. I said I didn't need help. I hadn't remembered that I had suffered a stroke and I was completely shocked when I saw a wheelchair in the corner of the room. I then noticed that my left arm didn't work – further bewilderment – what was happening? I didn't know what day, month or even year it was. I learned that I was in the Algonquin Hotel, New York, and I was directing JT Rogers' *The Overwhelming*. But why? I had already directed it in London. Stella tells me I demanded to know why on earth I'd be doing it again. She answered ruefully, 'I really don't know.'

I was still trying to piece my life together at this point, and while I knew I loved Stella I had no idea what our relationship was. I tried what I thought was a masterful piece of tact: 'Are you my girlfriend or my wife?' 'Well, I'm sort of both,' she said carefully. I thought it best to resolve this matter immediately: 'Well, I think we should get married as soon as I get my mind back,' I offered. And once again I began the same cycle of questions: 'Where am I? What am I doing here?' Apparently I asked the same questions for the next 12 hours. In any case, a car was called and I was admitted to the Presbyterian Cornell Hospital, where I met you.

Over the next 12 hours my memory began to return, or perhaps, more accurately, it was recalibrated. Stella began by teaching me the names of the cast, and as their names became familiar, faces and the roles they were playing swam into my perception. During the four days I was in the Presbyterian Cornell my memory recovered completely and there appeared to be no side effects. I was prescribed heparin, a blood thinner, to prevent the recurrence of any stroke, and you stopped by daily to monitor my recovery and provide a reassuring neurological presence.

Though my memory had largely returned, I was still in a state of post-traumatic shock. There was a very real possibility that I was no longer fit to continue rehearsal. Indeed, this was clearly an option the Roundabout Theatre management were exploring, and at one point they offered the job to Stella. I owed much not simply to Stella's support, and yours, but also to the steadfast constancy and advocacy of JT Rogers, who was convinced that I could recover sufficiently to resume rehearsal.

So it proved, and I returned almost straight away to rehearse for half of each day. My assistant, Johanna (Jojo) Gruenhut, whom you met, had very capably taken over during my hospitalisation and she took rehearsals for the other half-day. I asked the Roundabout management to elevate Jojo to the status of Co-Director, or at least Associate Director. They refused. I insisted, but they were adamant. I have no idea why they continued on such an unfair course, but possibly it infringed Equity regulations, or it might have triggered financial complications. But the truth is that the Assistant Director is very far down the food chain in the New York theatre hierarchy. Customarily the replacement or understudy rehearsals are conducted by the Stage Manager in a mode reminiscent of the Staff Director in opera rehearsals. A typical direction might be: 'No, you pick up the coffee and then you walk five steps to the table and put it down again.' It does little to nurture young talent. Jojo Gruenhut has gone on to pursue a successful career in theatre.

In the course of our daily conversations I learned that you had been in Rwanda for some months following the genocide and had become involved in counselling both victims and perpetrators. Of course it was simply a coincidence that *The Overwhelming* was set in Rwanda, immediately before the genocidal attacks on the Tutsis in 1994, but in my brain-stunned state my capacity for amazement was drained and I accepted your knowledge of Rwanda as a perfectly logical and serendipitous event.

As soon as I started rehearsals again I invited you to come and talk to the cast, and you provided the actors with an invaluable range of first-hand insights. I remember one particular event you described: a Hutu who dreamt that his machete turned into a blade of grass, thus preventing him from killing a Tutsi acquaintance from the same village. In the course of the rehearsals you moved from being a professional consultant to becoming a good friend.

Six months after we had returned to London you rang me to say that you were taking time off to write a book and that you intended to devote one chapter to the process of rehearsing a play. With this in mind you asked if you could attend rehearsals of the next play I was directing. A few months later I started rehearsals for Stella's *Dreams of Violence*, with you in attendance for the first three weeks of rehearsal.

The characters included a recovering alcoholic, a teenage drug addict, an elderly gentleman with early cognitive decline and a woman with a hypertrophic (enlarged) heart who had a heart attack in the course of the play. After a week your presence seemed so essential that I could no longer imagine how I had ever got through rehearsals without a medical expert in attendance. In the final scene, Hildy, played by Catherine Russell, has had a heart attack and is in hospital recuperating. Her anxious family have gathered by her bed. It was an excellent dramatic device by Stella to bring all the characters and their storylines together. You told us that the first 24 hours following a heart attack were crucial to the patient. There could be a complete recovery, partial recovery or there could be a relapse and a second, possibly fatal, heart attack.

With this in mind, and to emphasise the insecurity and tension for the family, I passed Catherine a playing card, unseen by me or the rest of the cast. If it was a red card, Catherine would recover in the course of the scene. The higher the card the greater her recovery would be. But if it was a black card her condition would worsen, a black nine or 10 leading to a coma and Hildy's unfortunate demise. None of us knew what the outcome would be. It was a black seven, and Catherine's condition grew palpably worse as the improvisation progressed. It was time for medical intervention and I asked if you would join the improvisation and see if you could save her. You shot into the middle of the room and took charge immediately. 'Nurse, crash trolley, *now*!' you commanded. 'Dr Kieran, two micrograms atropine intravenous. Go! Mr Cooper, could you monitor the fluids, please.' The company drew on their *Casualty* or *Holby City* experience and there was a swirl of purposeful activity. I secretly slipped Catherine a second randomly chosen card: 'If it's a red card D saves you, but if it's a black card I'm afraid it's bad news.' Within seconds Catherine began a harrowing death rattle and expired within three minutes. The actors were stunned into immobility, but you turned to me sadly and said, 'Gee, Max, I'm so sorry. I've lost the patient.' It was a hilarious climax to a most instructive afternoon.

In 2014 I was in New York once again, directing Tom Kilroy's version of *The Seagull*, set in County Galway in 1878. Once again I turned to you for help, and you gave a full session of analysis to Isabel Desmond (Arkadina, played by Trudie Styler) and to Constantine (played by Slate Holmgren), who in Tom's version had had a breakdown in his first year at Trinity. This was extraordinarily helpful. You also expanded our understanding of, and gave detail to, Tom Kilroy's belief that a form of low-level depression gripped almost all of the characters.

You also supervised a surgery conducted in the village by Dr Hickey (Dr Dorn in Chekhov's original) who had at his disposal only the remedies and prescriptions available to an Irish country doctor in the 1870s. The remainder of the cast were patients who had been briefed by you on a wide variety of ailments and conditions. Dr Hickey is a Catholic and I had already learned that University College Dublin had opened its medical school in 1855, so Dr Hickey could well have been one of its first graduates. In one line he declares: 'I've delivered more babies than anyone else this side of the Shannon.' This marked the wholesale change from female midwives to male doctors that happened in gynaecology in Ireland at this time. We were all shocked by the limited range of medical options available to poor Dr Hickey: an accident with a pitchfork led to a gangrenous foot and necessitated an amputation, while poor hygiene and the absence of running water made childbirth extremely hazardous, despite Dr Hickey's most determined interventions.

Tom Kilroy's version of *The Seagull* always rendered me much happiness. I had first directed it at the Royal Court in 1981 with an extraordinary cast that included Alan Rickman, Harriet Walter, Anna Massey, TP McKenna and Tony Rohr. Revisiting the play in New York in 2014 was enormously enjoyable, and your presence provided added pleasure.

On a couple of occasions in my early years at Trinity I had stayed at John Huston's palatial Anglo-Irish country house, St Clerans, in exactly that part of County Galway where Tom had reset the play. Far from estranging the audience from Chekhov's Russian original, Tom's sensitive adaptation provided a recognisable and intimate set of social and cultural references that fully released Chekhov's humanity and humour. Both countries had a large peasantry, an almost non-existent middle-class and a decaying aristocracy. And both were on the brink of a transforming revolution. Turgenev had acknowledged these affinities when he wrote: 'I could never have written about the Russian peasantry as I did had I not read Maria Edgeworth.'

Stella and I have between us many good friends in the theatre world – writers, actors, designers, stage managers – and they have been extremely supportive over the past three years. But neither of us has many intimate friends outside this magic circle. A high-flying lawyer, an artist and an art curator are about the whole of it. And that is just one reason why I place such value on our continued friendship, which has grown stronger over the 12 years we have known each other, despite the 3,000 miles that usually separate us.

With love and every best wish,
Max

DIRECTORS

William Gaskill, June 24, 1930–February 4, 2016, was a seminal theatre director who brought Brechtian principles, clarity and rigour to his productions. He was the second Artistic Director of the Royal Court from 1965 to 1972. Bill was one of a number of extraordinarily talented lieutenants who worked with George Devine in the earliest days of the English Stage Company at the Royal Court. Bill, John Dexter, Lindsay Anderson, Anthony Page and Peter Gill had rather different political inclinations.

Lindsay was very much to the right of the group and had a groundless fear that the Royal Court was being taken over by Marxists, while Bill was very much to the radical left. He was unperturbed by experiment and his regime at the Royal Court hosted a festival of alternative theatre called Come Together. However, all these directors shared a deep belief in the seriousness of theatre. George Devine memorably said, 'You should choose your theatre as carefully as you do your religion'. They were all influenced by the uncluttered clarity of the Berliner Ensemble, and Jocelyn Herbert was the designer of choice for most of them.

Bill had a musical passion and he loved the ballet. He paid attention to the rhythm, cadence and punctuation of the speech, and I believe a great part of his frustration came about when the actor did not hear the same tune. He had a grace, allied with an intuitive political sensibility that he shone like a searchlight to illuminate the text he was working on. This last is a rare attribute; many young directors may be politically engaged but are unable to apply this to their work. The combination of these talents together with a clarity of purpose and an unremitting rigour made Bill not simply a good director but a great one.

June 12, 2019

Dear Bill,

I think about you a lot and I miss you. Perhaps it's the time of year. I am writing at the beginning of June and you always gave a party in your flat in Leighton Road on the Sunday in mid-June that was nearest to your birthday and to Midsummer's Day. The cast list was unvaried. Pauline Melville, Ken Cranham, Peter Gill, Anthony Page, Paul Freeman, Susan Engel, Catherine Freeman, Jennie Stoller, Philip Arditti, Nadia Latif, Wunmi Mosaku, Caryl Churchill, Lenore Robinson, Eve Pearce, as well as your friends from Texas, Patrick and Judy Kelly, if they were in town. We were not a close group. Often I hadn't seen the others since the previous year's party. The food was always excellent and was usually served by a group of your ex-students from RADA.

I wouldn't describe you as a father figure. After all, most of the time I knew you I had a perfectly good father of my own. And yet... during the '80s the Royal Court had an exchange programme with Joseph Papp's Public

Theater in New York. I directed there several times and got to know Joe quite well. His office was in a separate building from the four theatres and the rehearsal room, and it became a habit to gather there after rehearsal for a glass of wine and a chat.

I liked Joe enormously and thought he was a terrific producer. Like you, he was extremely well read and could talk at length on Shakespeare, O'Casey, Broadway, Mayor Ed Koch or Meryl Streep. Often the evening ended with dinner in one of the excellent restaurants around Astor Place. The evenings functioned in providing the stimulating and challenging seminars that university had promised but never quite delivered. On the first occasion that Joe came to London I was eager for the two of you to meet and I invited you both to dinner at La Poule au Pot, an old haunt of yours around the corner from the Royal Court. The evening did not go well. You snapped at each other like a pair of bad-tempered elderly lions. Shakespeare was a particular bone of contention. You thought Joe's ideas shallow and populist, while he considered you to be dry and academic. When we next met you said, 'Max, it's no use introducing your father figures to each other. We're not going to get on, you know.'

You and I agreed to collaborate and work together in the course of a conversation sitting on the steps of the Royal Court Theatre in the summer of 1972. I had just finished work with the Traverse Workshop Company, who had completed a brief season at the Theatre Upstairs. This had involved collaboration with Bread, Love and Dreams, a folk-rock band and had really marked the end of my American-influenced hippie theatre experiments. And you had finished your term as Artistic Director of the Royal Court. Both of us were ready for new ideas. It was never an equal partnership: you were far more accomplished and experienced than I was, as well as being 12 years older. As for me, I knew enough to know that I didn't know very much. But I think the collaboration went better and was more fun than either of us had anticipated.

I had seen Grotowski's group perform on a series of dining-room tables, with the audience sitting at their feet, and various weird shows that enforced an intimate audience involvement at the Mickery Theatre in Holland. So I brought to the partnership an enthusiasm for experiment, while you brought both a more sophisticated political sensibility and intellectual rigour.

We agreed to start with a workshop on Heathcote Williams' book, *The Speakers*, about the eccentric speakers at Hyde Park Corner. In a three-week concentrated workshop actors are able to learn almost anything. In Denmark the Traverse Workshop Company had learned to walk on a slack rope four feet off the ground. On this occasion the actors learned to speak extempore on any subject picked at random – from traffic wardens to the Albigensian Heresy. We agreed we both wanted to take the work further, and I think I had the idea to stage it as a promenade piece. You developed the idea by focusing the action around a central scaffolding tower which had a lighting rig but also acted as a tea stall, where Jennie Stoller and subsequently Cecily Hobbs presided, selling cups of tea and cakes to the punters during the performance.

We edited Heathcote's book into overlapping scenes and speeches. There were no seats and this forced the audience to choose which event they wished to follow.

You were liberated from the fierce hold of the proscenium arch and your invention developed the concept. The actors learned to cope with hecklers and became so vigorous and foul-mouthed in quelling any audience interpolations that they had to be restrained. But in Dublin we got into trouble. A late-night performance at the Abbey Theatre with both actors and audience on the stage, and in which the rules of engagement between the two had already been deliberately broken, inevitably led to trouble. The audience had already had a few jars after seeing earlier performances and were in a merry mood and ready to take the actors on in verbal exchanges. The word quickly spread through the Dublin Theatre Festival, and one night the performance was dignified by the attendance of the distinguished Irish President, Cearbhall Ó Dálaigh. During the performance two audience members pissed loudly and copiously on the back wall. At this point the President's two armed guards decided that the President had seen enough and escorted him offstage and through the auditorium, accompanied by jeers and catcalls from the rest of the audience. Next day we apologised to the Abbey's Artistic Director, Thomas MacAnna. He was unfazed. 'Sure, this is the Abbey,' he said. 'We're used to riots here.'

Our second co-production was David Hare's adaptation of *Fanshen*, William Hinton's account of the advent and complications of bringing communism to a small Chinese village. In the course of the rehearsals I absorbed a methodology from you which I have adapted and used ever since. Again we started with a workshop in which I recall we drank a lot of tea and had many discussions on how to walk on bound feet. More usefully, we applied the principles of Fanshening or 'turning over' to ourselves. Your flat and your income meant you were rated as a 'middle peasant' and we were to liberate your assets and divide them between the group. We also decided that Ken Cranham be disciplined for wishing to leave the group and play Hal in *Henry IV Part One* in Nottingham. We deemed that the tavern scenes were frivolous and indulgent. 'Well, I do hope we're not going to begin with a lot of peasants hoeing?' he countered. We denied this vigorously, but of course in the end *Fanshen* began with just that: a scene in which a long line of peasants were hoeing.

We split the scenes between us and divided the work. One day you allocated me a fairly straightforward scene to direct. The peasants had already overcome the tyrannical landlords and were dividing their possessions between them. The ex-landlords protested at this and were beaten by the peasants. One of the actors, Roderick Leigh, had developed a nice line in cowering, browbeaten peasantry and protested that he was too abject and cowardly to dare assault his former masters. Psychologically he had a point, but I had watched you working and had fully understood for the first time that what determined the scene could by no means be decided simply by the character's personality but by the writer's overall purpose for the scene. In this case, unless the peasants bullied and beat the landlords they would not turn them into inveterate counter-revolutionaries who would then threaten the whole process. In the second half of the play the peasants would accept that they had gone too far and that some restitution had to be made. Thus the task of the actors was not to find reasons why their peasants would refrain from violence but to discover how each of them could go too far in doing so.

I armed each of the peasants with a rolled-up broadsheet newspaper to use as a stick or club. This is useful because if you strike someone as hard as you can with a rolled-up newspaper it causes no hurt but it makes a satisfying thwack and gives the illusion of serious assault. (NB: do not strike the face or unclothed arms and legs.) The actors embraced this idea and after a few tentative prods with the newspaper Roderick's peasant launched into a furious attack on the tyrannous landlords that spoke of exploding rage and frustration, bottled up by years of subjugation. It was lunchtime, but unseen by us you had wandered into the rehearsal room to watch the last 15 minutes. You were due to take the afternoon session. 'That's excellent work,' you said. 'You must carry on this afternoon and I'll go to an exhibition.' Of course, your imprimatur gave me great confidence.

Our third and final collaboration for Joint Stock was *Yesterday's News*, which was my introduction to verbatim plays. There had been a nine-day-wonder newspaper story about a group of mercenaries in Angola. An ex-army sergeant, who named himself Colonel Callan, had recruited a squad of ex-soldiers and had made up the numbers with a couple of labourers from a building site and two schoolboys. Of course they were untrained and, unsurprisingly, some of them ran away when attacked by the enemy. Colonel Callan shot several of them for deserting. This was the story that was making front-page headlines. One of the actors, Paul Kember, had worked as a journalist on the *Liverpool Echo*. Through his detective skills and a considerable stroke of luck, we were able to locate the recruiter of the mercenaries, who worked from the Tower Hotel. Subsequently, through a friendly and loquacious taxi driver, we also found two of the mercenaries who had been in Angola. We had the story every journalist in London was seeking.

David Rintoul and I met the mercenaries in a pub up the road from where we were rehearsing. We told them we were working with a group of actors and were keen to talk to them about their experiences. Their readiness to talk diminished considerably when they learnt that we were not a film company and had no money. After a drink, David and I returned to the rehearsal room somewhat despondently. 'Maybe they'll come, maybe they won't,' we told the group. It was just before Christmas and the actors were huddled in a circle around the stove in a corner of a decrepit rehearsal room. Suddenly the door burst open and in came the two mercenaries. The chunky one, who had been a paratrooper, came straight over and stood in the middle of our circle. Meanwhile the lean and lanky one, who had been in the SAS, strode round the hall kicking open the exit doors. It was freezing. He came over to join his mate, saying politely to us, 'So, ya wanna talk?' We all sat down and for two hours they talked and we listened.

They told us about the intricacies of laying an electronic ambush so that it would cause the maximum possible damage. 'Let's say you put an explosive on a jungle path. Your adversaries turn around and run back the way they've come but 100 yards back down the path is a second charge. This splits and panics the party, who dash left and right into the bush, where of course there are further charges 50 yards into the bush.' And how to make reluctant Irish terrorists talk: 'You blindfold Paddy, take him up to 200 feet. Take the blindfold off and shove his head out the door. Pull him back inside, put the blindfold on again, take the chopper down to two feet off the ground and push him out. Paddy is shitting himself by now and would betray his granny in a flash.' It was fascinating – albeit highly politically incorrect. The chunky one came from Walthamstow, as did Will Knightley, one of the actors. Both had played for the same junior football team and bonded over their Walthamstowian experience.

After *Yesterday's News* you and I went our separate ways with Joint Stock. I directed *Light Shining in Buckinghamshire* (*LS in B*) by Caryl Churchill, and then you directed *A Mad World, My Masters*, by Barrie Keeffe, in 1977, and *The Ragged-Trousered Philanthropists* in 1978. Firstly you obtained excellent adaptations from Barrie Keeffe and Stephen Lowe respectively. Both productions emphasised how powerful the Joint Stock ensemble had become and justified all the work and the hours that had gone into making that standard of work possible. *A Mad World, My Masters* was also very, very funny and showed you in full command of a broad vein of satire not readily associated with your work.

We stayed friends for the next 45 years. There was a hiatus in our friendship when I cancelled Ken Loach's production of *Perdition* at the Royal Court. You resigned from the Royal Court's council and we didn't speak for a year. We were both extremely relieved when we made up. You referred to the event only once: 'You see, Max,' you said, 'there will always be excellent and compelling reasons why a particular play should be cancelled. But it will never be the correct decision. It's simply not in the job description. Your role as Artistic Director of the Royal Court is to champion every play you choose.' I should pass this advice on to my successors.

Over the years I have collaborated with other directors and have always enjoyed and learned from the experience. Of course, as one gets older you have to turn the corner and learn from younger people. But I have never again learnt so much or worked with such purpose as I did in those three years with you.

I would have liked to have found out how you coped with not directing very much at all for the last 25 years of your life. I asked you directly once if you missed it. 'No,' you said sharply. 'Not in the least.' Well, I haven't directed for three years and miss it enormously, perhaps because working in the rehearsal room brings out a more open and generous side of me less visible in other contexts. And to paraphrase Andrew Marvell:

The grave is fine and most select,
But none I think do there direct.

The last major production of yours outside Joint Stock that I recall was *Armstrong's Last Goodnight*, at the Lyceum Theatre in Edinburgh in September 1976. I arrived in Edinburgh to do *LS in B* while you were in rehearsal. At the Traverse I bumped into Kenny Ireland, the Artistic Director of the Lyceum and a Joint Stock alumnus. I asked him how rehearsals were going. 'Ach weil,' he said, 'Bill had an actor in tears by half-past ten, and by half-past eleven he was in tears himself.' I recently met a distinguished elderly Irish actor who still trembled with aggrieved rancour when recalling rehearsals with you 35 years earlier at the Royal Court. And Simone Signoret, by then an elderly retired lady, when interviewed by *Harpers* or *Vogue*, was asked if she missed work and became depressed. 'Of course there are bad days,' she said. 'But on the worst days I think at least I am not at the Royal Court Theatre rehearsing *Macbeth* with William Gaskill.'

I think what frustrated you most acutely was the impossibility of fusing a disparate group of actors into an ensemble in the standard four-week rehearsal period customarily afforded by British theatres. Your iconic ideal was the Berliner Ensemble, and there were only three occasions in your working life when conditions approached the continental norm. These were the initial period of your time as Artistic Director at the Royal Court, when you had a permanent company. Then there was your time with Joint Stock, when for 18 months we had a permanent company.

And finally there was your work at RADA. I believe that the frustration and disappointment at what you were able to achieve outweighed any pleasure or satisfaction. I did not set the same exacting standards. But I do recall a question-and-answer session in St Petersburg with Russian directing students. 'What are English actors paid?' one of them asked. I replied, '£300 pounds a week,' or whatever the equity rate was at the time. This seemed an astronomical sum to them. I was then asked how long actors rehearsed for in England. When I replied that four weeks was the norm, the interpreter did not understand. 'Did you mean to say four months or four years?' he asked uncomprehendingly.

I know you painted and that you attended a poetry course at the City Lit. Indeed one of your pictures, an imitation of *Jesus Being Taken Down from the Cross*, hangs on our wall. It is very precise and detailed, but it has an imaginative fluidity.

And what do I do? Well, I read a lot. For example, in the past year I have read almost everything that has been published about the Irish Famine of 1846. I had hoped to find a scheme for a play, but it is probably too epic and too grim.

About two years before you died I was reviving *Our Country's Good* and I persuaded you to work on some scenes. We agreed on the scenes and the next morning I left you to it. Arriving in the rehearsal room for the mid-morning coffee break, I was alarmed to discover that you were just on the second paragraph of the first speech. After the break you started again at the beginning. The actor playing Captain Phillip was the excellent John

Hollingworth, who had been a student of yours at RADA and was not too intimidated by you. He got as far as the first paragraph. 'Is that any better, Bill?' he enquired hopefully. 'No, no, John. Not in the slightest,' was your candid response. Yet in the course of the morning the punctuation and the phrasing were rigorously examined, together with the sense and rhetoric of Captain Phillip's speech, and in the course of a long run John's delivery never coarsened or became too expansive.

The final occasion we talked together about work was when you came to a performance of *Our Country's Good* at the St James Theatre. At least you didn't walk out, but you found the performances overheated and overwrought. As I drove you home you said, 'I don't suppose we had as much in common as we thought at the time,' ruefully referring to our years in Joint Stock together. 'But some very good work came of it and we must be thankful for that,' you concluded magisterially. It was a fitting epitaph.

I would only add that on reflection I realise that we also had an extraordinary synchronicity of taste. You have directed rather more classics than I have, but without any preplanning or prior discussion we have both directed *Macbeth*, *The Recruiting Officer*, *Three Sisters*, *The Man of Mode*, *All That Fall* and *She Stoops to Conquer*. So perhaps we had quite a lot in common. At any rate I like to think so.

With much love,

Max

Danny Boyle today, of course, is a national icon. His extraordinary four-hour opening ceremony that heralded the London Olympics in 2012 set out to celebrate a surprisingly diverse and particular range of British achievements that included the Industrial Revolution, the NHS, the Queen and James Bond. It was unforgettable. Many of the qualities he exhibited had been present in Danny as a young man. In a recent *Guardian* article Danny says, 'I believe in the inherent goodness of human beings.' The article also cites his faith in 'art and industry'. His ideals are a bedrock, or perhaps a guiding light through the gloom.

Danny worked for Joint Stock as an assistant stage manager in 1978. He joined me at the Royal Court as an assistant director in 1981. I remember him as fresh-faced and enthusiastic, with a coherent political sensibility impressive in one so young. In Royal Court script meetings he championed a Polish play by Tadeusz Glowacki and pressured me to programme it in the Theatre Upstairs. I thought the play a bit ponderous, but I had already learned that it is often a wise choice to surrender to the enthusiasm of younger colleagues. Danny did a thorough and painstaking job, and in retrospect I see that it marked the beginning of the Royal Court's important international commitment.

Certainly he had talent, but it was his integrity, positivity and determination that were his outstanding qualities as a young man. He directed *Victory, Saved, The Grace of Mary Traverse* Downstairs, and *Salonika* Upstairs before leaving the Royal Court in 1985.

I put Danny up for a Regional Theatre Young Director's Scheme bursary for three successive years. On each occasion he failed to make a shortlist. To fail once was understandable, twice was myopic on behalf of the adjudicators and thrice was inexcusable. Danny Boyle is the most successful failure ever. The letter below is dated early 1982, a year or so after both of us had started working at the Royal Court.

January 28, 1982

Dear Danny,

I was so sorry to hear that you had been turned down yet again for the Regional Theatre Young Director scheme. Like you, some years ago I also came seventh and failed to make the cut for a BBC Trainee Scheme. These things don't signify a great deal and I am very thankful today to be working for the Royal Court and not the BBC. I remember discussing your prospects with Bill Gaskill at the time you left Joint Stock and telling him you wanted to direct. 'You never know,' he said. 'You just have to push them out of the nest and see if they fly.' In the hope that you will soar, the Royal Court will renew your contract for another year, which will enable you to get on with the Glowacki play. You have determination, ambition, and you like actors. These seem to me three of the most important attributes for a director. Above all, I think that directing is a pragmatic skill acquired more readily in the rehearsal room than the lecture hall.

There are many ways of directing and you will pick up skills from the directors you observe, and of course there are other diverse sources which will enable you. Here are some of the fellas who helped me. When I first worked at the Traverse in 1966 the Chairman of the theatre's board was Tom Mitchell, who among other properties owned the lease of the theatre building in the Lawnmarket. I should have disapproved of a property developer, but in fact I liked him enormously. He came from a farming family in Cumbria and was also Chairman of Workington Town rugby league club. During the war he had apparently been Commandant of a camp for German prisoners of war and had been manager of the first Great Britain rugby league team to win a series in Australia.

I stayed in flats he owned in Marchmont Road, Danube Street and in West Bow. He was pleasingly casual about the rent. Over dinner one evening he would say, 'I think it's about time you paid me some money.' I would give him a cheque for a fairly random sum and he would never say if it was sufficient or insufficient. But the most exciting of his properties was a semi-derelict country house at Gorebridge, in East Lothian, named Harvieston Hall. I don't really remember, but it must have had gas and water or it would have been a health hazard. I think it had been squatted before Tom acquired it because there were colourful graffiti over most of the bedroom walls. Tom encouraged a group of us, mainly actors, to stay there, probably to stop it being squatted any further. In a garage at the back of the house there were two pre-war Rolls-Royces. Both were filthy but otherwise in pretty good condition. I never saw Tom drive them, or even attempt to start them, but I did spot him once or twice unlocking the garage and peering at them proudly.

The most exciting feature, however, was a meadow at the front of the house, which sloped down to a railway line. This was the Waverly route from Edinburgh to Carlisle via Hawick and Galashiels that had been abandoned one year earlier, despite the efforts of David Steel. However, a stub of the line from Edinburgh to Gorebridge remained open to serve some collieries. The occasional steam train would majestically puff by at the bottom of the meadow. It was almost like having your own private railway.

I bonded with Tom over rugby and he came to see me play for Edinburgh Wanderers a couple of times. On one occasion we drove down to Cumbria to see Workington Town play. On the way back we hatched a plan. He would speak to the coach and next week I would play for Workington Town Reserves against Barrow. I enjoyed the game. There was a great deal of tackling involved as I recall. It was difficult to adjust to the slightly different rules and to stay in the right position as scrum half. In fact this led to the crowning moment in my 80-minute career as a rugby league player. I was out of position, covering rather haphazardly behind the Town three-quarter line and in a position to field a cunning little chip over the top from the Barrow fly half. I successfully ran the ball back 30 yards before being smacked to the ground by two or three beefy Barrow players. After the game I received much spirited advice from my fellow players about contracts and signing-on fees. Driving back the next day Tom made me a promise. 'If you've got a good idea, come to me,' he said, 'and I'll see what I can do.' I said I didn't have a good idea at that moment. 'No matter,' he said. 'It takes 25 seconds to have a good idea but it may take 25 years to put it into practice.' I never took Tom up on this offer, but perhaps I was like the Rolls-Royces in the garage, destined to be peered at from time to time but never taken out and driven.

The point is, really, Danny, that you will occasionally meet wealthy men or women like Tom, for whom the theatre is an interesting and eccentric hobby. If you do cleave to them, what they really want is your company. When all's said and done, being a property developer is probably pretty dull work, and Tom said that keeping Workington Town afloat cost the Mitchell family 'three separate fortunes'. But he liked having a theatre as well as a rugby league club in his portfolio and I will always remember it only takes 25 seconds to have a good idea.

Directors will at first be the biggest influence on you, and you have already seen that there are many different ways to go about things. John Dexter famously liked to stage the play straight away and have a run-through at the end of the first week, while Bill is much more fastidious about phrasing and punctuation than me. One early mentor for me was Tom O'Horgan, the Director of the La Mama Troupe and the first Director of *Hair*. The physicality and musicianship of his actors was impressive.

He had a bit of a temper too, and he used to shout at the actors. On one occasion he shouted and threw a mug at one of them. He missed and the mug hit a radiator at the side of the room, making a range of different notes as it struck the different bars. He liked the sound so much that when the mug was returned to him he shied it again. This time, of course, he missed the radiator and hit the actor, causing much hilarity.

I thought losing one's temper was essential to being a good director. I tried it several times and it was Tony Rohr who approached me in a coffee break and said, 'Leave it out, Max. It's totally unconvincing. Nobody believed you.' I realised that day that I would never be a shouter.

Susan Williamson was in the first ever professional play I directed at the Traverse. I used to drive her home every night after rehearsal. She gave me a lot of pragmatic advice about staging and costume, but the most important lesson I absorbed as a young director is that the actors are your friends and allies and not your opponents. They are a collective repository of wisdom and experience you can draw from. But you know this already. I have seen you with actors and they know you are not frightened of them. This is the great obstacle for young directors.

Susan was an enabler. So too was Mildred Dunnock, who was the first Linda Loman in *Death of a Salesman*. I directed her in Pinero's *Trelawny of the Wells* at the Long Wharf Theatre in New Haven, Connecticut. She was American theatrical royalty. She was married to a prosperous Wall Street banker who, quite rightly, treated Mildred as a national treasure. She was delivered by her chauffeur to rehearsal every morning at 10am. He would pick her up again every evening to negotiate the perilous Connecticut winter roads. She was a brilliant Mrs Telfer. The Telfers had formerly been leading actors at the Wells. Mr Telfer has been offered a line of small parts while Mrs Telfer is to be the wardrobe mistress. She does, however, have the best lines in the play. 'They have pushed us from our stools, just as some other new fashion, in the course of time, will push them from their stools... if we are set to scrub a floor – and it may come to that yet, let us make up our minds to scrub it legitimately and with dignity.'

It was a large cast, about 18, I think. My excellent agent, Peter Murphy, of Curtis Brown, had not revealed to Arvin Brown, the long-serving Director of the Long Wharf, that I had never previously directed a play with a cast larger than five. After the first run-through I turned, notebook in hand, to address a bleacher full of actors. I started by giving Mildred an anodyne, and I'm sure not very helpful, note: 'That is an excellent note. Max, thank you. I'm going to write that down,' she proclaimed in patrician tones. Mildred unclasped her leather handbag and produced a new notebook and a gold propelling pencil. 'Thank you so much,' she said again, and turned to make sure that her exemplary behaviour had been observed by the rest of the cast. Of course my confidence grew.

I learned a further lesson from *Trelawny of the Wells*. There was another famous actor in the play: John Bakos was nationally known from the Shake 'n Bake television commercials. He was a clown, really, and he played the comedian in the Wells company. He devised an extended piece of comic business. I don't recall it in detail, but it involved signing a contract, getting ink on his fingers and transferring it to a piece of bread he was eating at the same time. I thought it heavy-handed and coarse and did my best to discourage John, without having the courage to confront him directly. On the first preview it provoked screams of laughter and I realised I was completely wrong. This was a hilarious, appropriate and valuable piece of business. The lesson here is that genius comes in many different guises. You may not recognise it at first but when you do, clasp it firmly to you.

You may well have the opportunity from time to time to work with someone super-talented. Often they may be stars. There are many talented actors who are not stars, but in my experience, few stars who are not very talented. These too should be embraced. Not only will you learn from these people but they will dignify and elevate your work. They will make an ordinary director seem good and a good director appear excellent. I have been lucky and privileged to have worked with Stanley Eveling, Caryl Churchill, David Hare and Howard Brenton, amongst others. I also want to tell you about Rachel Roberts and Donal McCann – both have excellent taste and an unnervingly accurate self-appraisal of their own capabilities. Both are proud without being vain and both have judgement without being judgemental. Both select the good notes while fending off the poor ones without offence. It is always humbling but not humiliating to work with people with talent superior to one's own. They are your enablers.

I must also mention my father, David, who was a leading psychiatrist and author. He also had a certain theatricality which he used in his lectures and in the highly successful television programmes he fronted. He very much approved of a career in the theatre and gave me every encouragement. He came to every production I did at the Royal Court, just as earlier he came to every rugby match I played in. I drove him back to his home in Dulwich one night after he had seen *Cloud 9*. It was just after he had retired. I stopped the car outside the house and he said, 'You are now much busier than your mother and me. That probably means that we will want to see you much more than you are able to see us, but always remember how much we love you.' As he opened the car door, he said, 'I don't know exactly what it is that you do as a director but I do know that you do it extremely well.' It was a tremendous moment, and I could easily say the same of you.

So, very good luck, and remember that the best method is your method, whatever that may be, and you will arrive at it by doing it.

Support comes in unexpected packaging – be open to surprise.

Best wishes,

Keep in touch.

As ever, with great affection and respect,

Max

Rufus Norris is the fourth Artistic Director of the National Theatre. He has been a staunch advocate of new work. *London Road* was one of his great successes.

February 8, 2019

Dear Rufus,

In a recent article you stated that most directors who were candidates to work at the National were friends of yours. I don't think I am able to claim that privilege, although you have been very friendly and charming on the two occasions that we have met and once when we talked at length on the phone. Let me make it clear from the start that I am an admirer of your tenure at the National and particularly of your clear commitment to new and contemporary writing. I am also an admirer of your own directing and intend to take out a second mortgage and purchase two tickets for *Small Island*.

On one occasion a few years ago I was climbing the stairs to my office at Out of Joint when I was accosted by a young actress who was working with a company who had hired our rehearsal room. She told me how much she admired my work and how much she aspired to work with me. In particular she said she was thrilled by my production of *London Road*. Of course, I should have pointed out that if she wished to flatter her way into a job it should be accompanied by at least some rudimentary research. Instead, I think I accepted the compliment graciously and continued upstairs in a warm glow.

I have no idea if my admiration is in any way reciprocated, but at any rate you have recently programmed three plays at the National Theatre which I originally brought to the stage. These are *LS in B*, *Our Country's Good* and *Top Girls*. I admit that there is a competitive side to my nature that hoped these productions would not be so excellent that they would cloud the cherished memories and nostalgic recollections of my own productions. I fight the tendency as best I can but always recollect that Confucius wrote: 'There is no more pleasant sight than to see a good friend fall from a rooftop.' However, I was dismayed by all of these productions.

You took the bold and brave step of staging all three plays in the Lyttelton. But all had been created for a 400-seat theatre experiencing severe economic restraints, and their mode of presentation had been governed by what could be termed 'the aesthetics of poor theatre'. What does that mean? It means simple and carefully budgeted sets and, in each case, an ensemble of actors playing two or three parts each. The doubling was even commented on in the text of *Our Country's Good*, when Wisehammer objects to playing both Bullock and Captain Brazen in the convicts' production of *The Recruiting Officer*. 'It will confuse the audience,' he says. Timberlake had observed Ron Cook's very real misgivings, voiced in the course of rehearsals, and had incorporated them into the text.

Certainly when the capacity of a theatre exceeds 400 the demands of theatricality change: detail and ensemble playing become less important, and pageantry and epic staging are required. The drama tends to focus round the crisis and resolution in the life of a single leading character. Certainly there are advantages to staging new work in the Lyttelton: it confers status on the work, and with the National's excellent marketing department audiences would be satisfactory and the writers would earn significantly higher royalties.

But bigger doesn't necessarily mean better and one size definitely does not fit all. Clearly you recognised the particular demands, as the National provided the directors with two of the most exciting and innovative designers working in the country: Es Devlin and Ian Macneil. Yet Es's charismatic and eye-catching set for *LS in B* dominated the actors. Moreover, two of the three plays, *LS in B* and *Our Country's Good*, depict societies gripped by abject poverty, and the deployment of lavish theatrical resources seemed oddly inappropriate. All three plays employed extra actors with the obvious intention of populating the vasty wastes of the Lyttelton stage and depicting a whole society. I understand this is an old tactic, much used by Beerbohm Tree and Henry Irving in their Shakespeare seasons. However, if the audience are unable to discern either the identity or the function of the actors, they appear as a gaggle of unhappy commuters haplessly searching for a change of platform at Liverpool Street.

A better alternative in the case of *LS in B* might have been to celebrate the space, rather than attempt to populate it with people and furniture. In his book *Play Writing* Stephen Jeffreys writes about the scene in which the two peasant women debate what they might take from the farmer's house. One of them has entered the unlocked house and returns with a piece of mirror. Jeffreys writes: 'She [Caryl Churchill] fragments the language and pulls it back, not drawing attention to it when the actors need to take centre stage. She draws attention to the nakedness of the situation itself. In this scene the simplicity and power of the situation conducts our attention to the women on a bare stage with a piece of broken mirror. The language is plain because the situation is extreme and therefore doesn't require a great deal of heavy characterisation, or thought, or even comment [or scenery, I would add]. Churchill lets the scene speak for itself.' The very emptiness tells the story.

I don't know about your working methods. I expect, like mine, they're an accumulation rather than a philosophy. I use improvisations quite a lot in rehearsals, not so much for the characters, and very rarely for prompting narrative ideas, but usually to clarify the backstory or to dramatise offstage events. However, this scene from *LS in B* and *The Science of Hanging* from *Our Country's Good* are exceptions. Both were prompted by improvisations.

For the rehearsals of *LS in B* – or 'Lux in Bucks', as David Rintoul called it – we decided to work for a day on my uncle Wren's farm in Aston Clinton, Buckinghamshire. It was a sunny day in early May, the cattle had already been turned out into the meadows for the spring grass and the stackyard was empty. It was secluded and sheltered. Wren was working in the 16-acre field across the road and I knew that the Edwardian farmhouse at the top of the hill would be both empty and unlocked. Wren never locked it during the day. So I sent the three actresses up to the house with a mission to steal one item each. One took a blanket, one a copper watering can from above the kitchen range, and one liberated a shaving mirror from the upstairs bathroom. Of course, the items were returned before Wren finished work. The stolen mirror meant that the actress understood that her character could see her own face for the first time. Caryl developed this scene from the account of the improvisation as told by the actress as we sat in the secluded stackyard on a May afternoon in 1975.

I appreciate that I was encouraged and nurtured at various important stages of my career, and I appreciate that you are doing this in your turn, but meanwhile it would be good if you could encourage the young directors to focus more on the text and on realising the writer's intentions, rather than feeling that they have to perform directorial acrobatics, and that their creativity depends on adding extra elements. A great production of a poor play gives the playgoer enough to chew on, but a poor production of a great play makes one fulminate with Corneille. '*Ô rage! Ô désespoir!*' Putting plays with a political context into the hands of young directors unable to focus any beliefs they may hold on the play itself will erode and ultimately subvert the work.

I realise that in a highly saturated market theatre is competing with sophisticated television drama and with a constant stream of information from the internet. I understand that theatre must compete. However, there is a danger that we lose sight of the essential simplicity and directness that are theatre's most powerful assets.

Actually, forget these last paragraphs. They form a thinly disguised job application. So let's just regard this as a wee chat between friends.

Best wishes,

As ever,

Max

Cath Walsh is Head of Drama at Sacred Heart College, Merseyside. Her most recent productions include *Beauty and the Beast* and *A Midsummer Night's Dream.*

March 2, 2020

Dear Cath Walsh,

When talking to Ian Redford a couple of weeks ago he relayed a conversation you had had about how a handbook of 'actioning' would be of use to both teachers and students. I have just completed a book on a slightly different subject and will not be embarking on a new one in the near future. Writing is exhausting! However, there is a part of it which may be of help and I will try and summarise it in this letter!

Actioning may most usefully be described as a homemade version of Stanislavski's methodology. A version of actioning has long been taught in some drama schools (Drama Centre). It leads actors to elucidate what they want in a scene and to define the actions or tactics they use to achieve this. Each separate thought or tactic is defined by a transitive verb. Of course, everybody instinctively uses actions in everyday conversational exchanges, which is why I have chosen to focus on a conversation between the Prime Minister, Boris Johnson, and Andrew Marr which took place on *The Andrew Marr Show* on December 19, 2019. Each change of thought is defined by a transitive verb. So a sentence like 'I love you' is invalid because it is not transitive, but also, more importantly, because it defines the state of the speaker without guiding him or her towards any particular mode of delivery. But because the speaker is in a state of love, he or she may choose actions like 'flatters', 'praises', 'charms', 'interests', 'fascinates' and so on. Ideally the actors/students should select the actions themselves, as they will then commit to them more readily. But, in practice, as the director/teacher, I will have actioned the whole scene beforehand, so I am in a position to prompt thoughts. However, at this stage flexibility and negotiation is important and the teacher/director should be ready to further the actor's inclinations.

Here is the scene: Boris Johnson's overall objective is to pin the blame for everything on Jeremy Corbyn. Andrew Marr's objective is to expose Boris Johnson and to show that he, Andrew, is a trenchant and forensic political journalist. I have selected an action before each thought, but of course there are alternatives.

During the interview Andrew Marr asks Boris Johnson how many other convicted terrorists have been released without consequences early from prison in similar circumstances to the London Bridge attacker Usman Khan.

(See actions in brackets)

BJ: [awakens] But not in the case of this individual, because after all he had been sentenced [convinces]. He had been sentenced under the existing law in 2010. That was the reality [pressures] and you should acknowledge that.

AM: [prepares] Okay, let's look. Okay, [focuses] well, let's look at what happened to him.

BJ: [discourages] You can't go back retrospectively.

AM: [pins] Let's look at what happened to him in the last ten years. [engages] Where was he in the last ten years? [exposes] In the prison system, which has been—

BJ: [humours] Yes, he was.

AM: …pretty much [confronts] disastrous under the Conservatives. [focuses] Let's go through a few figures. [appals] Suicides under the Conservatives in the prison system up by 50%. [shocks] Assaults on staff tripled in that period. [shames] Prisoner-on-prisoner assaults doubled, self-harm more than doubled.

BJ: [mollifies] And that is why this new Conservative administration, Andrew, is [dazzles] putting £2.5 billion into our prison service—

AM: [corrects] It's not a new Conservative administration; [scorns] it is the Conservative Party which has been in power for ten years.

BJ: [awakens] But we take a different approach.

AM: [mocks] So it's not the Conservative Party that we should look back at?

BJ: [convinces] We take a different… I'm a new prime minster, [lectures] we take a different approach. [dazzles] We're putting £2.5 billion into our prisons. We want to have… [disgusts] and unlike Shami Chakrabarti we want to have an extra—

AM [challenges] Tories don't want to stuff the prison service then?

BJ: … [focuses] Can I tell you what we're doing? [enthuses] We want to have an extra 10,000 places, and the reason [persuades] that we are confident in our ability to do that is because we have a strong economy. [assures] We can manage the economy sensibly and we will not rack up public debt [convinces] while they would take a sledgehammer to the resilience of the UK economy.

AM: Okay, [dismisses] enough of all that. [pins] Do you know how many—

BJ: [enlists] You know the disaster the Labour Party would be.

AM: [corners] Do you know how many magistrates and crown courts you have closed as a party in the last ten years? [bullies] Do you know how many have been closed in England and Wales?

BJ: [mollifies] We will be making investments to the Criminal Justice system—

AM: [pursues] Do you know?

BJ: …[evades] Across the board. I can't give you a figure.

AM: Okay, [shocks] I'll tell you. [shames] It's nearly 300 magistrate and crown courts that you have closed as the Conservatives across the country. [confronts] It's an astonishing record.

BJ: [mollifies] We of course understand now is the time to make investments not just in the NHS, [impresses] not just in policing, as we are doing, not just in the education service, but also in our criminal justice system. We're putting more money into counter terror. [horrifies] Jeremy Corbyn wants to scrap MI5. MI5—

AM: [reprimands] No don't talk about that. [grips] I'm not interested in Jeremy Corbyn; I'm interested in you.

BJ: …[sobers] MI5 is responsible for keeping us safe.

AM [pins] I'm sorry. I'm interested…

BJ: [refocuses] MI5 monitors thousands of people, such as Usman Kahn.

AM: Okay, [corners] I'm interested in you and your record. [berates] The record on prisons is appalling. [pins] You mentioned the NHS. [shames] You have again a terrifyingly bad record on the NHS. [skewers] The highest number of patients on waiting lists ever. [shakes] The worst performance on record for treating people within 18 weeks. The worst A&E performance since targets began. [pursues] Missing targets again on cancer patients being seen. [confronts] That is a terrible record.

BJ: [diverts] The NHS is doing a fantastic job under terrific pressure, and I do not for one minute deny the pressure.

AM: [pins] All of those things are true, are they not?

BJ: I do not for one minute [evades] deny the pressure that the NHS is under, but that is why [impresses] we are so determined to make huge investments in the NHS. [dazzles] The largest—

AM: [punctures] But you haven't been telling the truth about those investments.

Make the actors/students proclaim the action before they say the line on each occasion for as long as it takes before they are truly playing the intention. At the same time the teacher/director should if necessary be prepared to change the action so that the script remains an accurate map of the journey of the scene.

I do hope this letter will be helpful, but Ian tells me he may be visiting you shortly and he is a terrific teacher who has an excellent grasp of the working method. He should be able to answer any further questions the students may have.

Best wishes,
Yours sincerely,
Max Stafford-Clark

Richard Demarco was one of the founding members of the Traverse Theatre and has been a constant innovator and influential presence on the Scottish art and wider cultural scene. He is himself a distinguished artist. I was asked to contribute to the Richard Demarco Archive, which is currently being digitalised to celebrate his 90th birthday.

20 June, 2020

Dear Ricky,

I learn it will be your 90th birthday on July 9th and I am writing to salute that happy event and to acknowledge with enormous gratitude your kindness and the unmerited encouragement you gave me when we first met 55 years ago. I was in Edinburgh on tour with Dublin University Rugby Club. I had been playing for the 2nd XV for most of the season but either somebody was injured or had pressing exam commitments (unlikely at Trinity, which had enjoyably relaxed academic requirements) and I made up the numbers as reserve scrum half and emergency full back. We had three fixtures: against Edinburgh University on Thursday (an easy win), Edinburgh Wanderers on Saturday (a narrow loss), and Edinburgh Academicals on Monday (an honourable draw).

But on the Sunday we had a day off, and that was when

I made my pilgrimage to the Traverse, about which I had read so much. Luckily for me, the Traverse has always been open on Sundays and I made my way down the narrow wynd of James Court for the first time and pushed open the rickety double doors at the bottom of the spiral stone staircase. It was like the entrance to a magic cave. About a dozen steps up, two doors were open and I was able to look into the hallowed theatre space where a stage manager was already setting props for the evening performance.

I continued to ascend and on the first floor the stairs opened out into a gallery with some rather finely detailed pen-and-ink drawings on the walls. I stepped in. At the far end you were squatting on the floor, supervising two young women who were stuffing flyers into envelopes. I was clearly intruding and began to retreat. You sprang to your feet and crossed the floor, saying, 'Welcome to the Traverse Art Gallery. Come in. I'm Ricky Demarco.' Within minutes I too was recruited to stuffing envelopes. It was the first of many occasions when I would undertake menial tasks on the Traverse's behalf. In the course of the afternoon I explained that I was directing a revue in the summer for Dublin University Players, and we were seeking a late-night slot in the early summer. To my amazement you were immediately enthusiastic about the idea and undertook to introduce me to Jim Haynes, the Traverse's artistic director. He also was welcoming.

The revue, *Dublin Fare*, was successful in its late-night slot and Jim followed up with the offer of similar programming in the Edinburgh Festival itself. This too was a success, helped by a glowing review by Mary Holland in

The Observer, and also by the fact that neither the Oxford nor the Cambridge revues were particularly strong that year. Buoyed by this success, *Dublin Fare* became part of the Traverse's celebratory season at the Jeannetta Cochrane Theatre in London. Here we met our demise. My limited directorial skills were quite unable to cope with either the cumbersome wooden set that was deemed necessary, or with the complex lighting plot, which on the first night stubbornly lagged one cue behind the action. Sketch after sketch remained in murky half-light while the scene changes were brilliantly illuminated. Milton Shulman of the *Evening Standard* wrote, 'The one good thing about this infantile undergraduate review is that none of these young people will ever be seen on the professional stage again.' On this last point he was decisively proved wrong, but he was right about almost everything else. So I had visited both Triumph and Disaster. They are now familiar destinations which I have called at on several occasions since.

So I was surprised when I got a call from you saying the Traverse was looking for a stage manager and you had suggested me to Jim. I think the salary was £12 a week. This was a considerable advance on the £5 I was then getting as a labourer on a local mushroom farm.

Undeniably I was the Traverse's most incompetent stage manager ever, but I was in the right place at the right time when Milo Sperber, a veteran RADA director, became ill and had to back out of rehearsals for Stanley Eveling's *Come and Be Killed*. I happily put my stage-management days behind me for ever, and with the guidance of the actors delivered a fairly competent production. You then persuaded a charming American academic, Bob Shure, to let me direct his short play, *Oh Gloria*.

The truth is that I knew little and could do less, but I was swept up by your tsunami of enthusiasm and for this I will remain for ever in your debt. Your ideas are always spontaneous, usually brilliant and have a delivery rate of about 50%. But these ideas have included the Traverse itself, the Ricky Demarco Gallery, the Demarco European Arts Foundation, a production of *Macbeth* in the middle of the Firth of Forth, and bringing Tadeusz Kantor and Joseph Beuys to Edinburgh. The energy, determination and stamina I needed to get through the three-week-long Edinburgh Festival always necessitated an immediate month's holiday, but you have maintained this cracking pace not just for 52 weeks, but for 52 weeks for well over 52 years.

Nor has it been easy. You have always been an exotic bird of paradise amidst the dun-coloured thrushes of lawyers, bankers and academics that constitute Edinburgh's intelligentsia. It may call itself the Athens of the North but, as we both know, Edinburgh is still a Presbyterian city. For example, when you wished to expand the size and the scope of the Traverse gallery and move to larger premises, Nicholas Fairbairn, the Conservative MP and criminal advocate, who was Chairman of the Traverse's board, prevented you from using the name, a mean-spirited gesture.

You recently told me how Mussolini's alliance with Hitler in 1940 provoked a wave of anti-Italian feeling in Edinburgh. You were called 'wops' and 'eyeties' and Churchill even proposed internment for Italian-Scots. I think you have probably had to withstand jealousy and antagonism from many different directions, and even from your own people. I recall an occasion when I had been to the cinema in Tollcross with Madeleine Maxwell-Arnott and walking back through the Grassmarket we stopped to pick up some chips from a fish and chip shop. We were conversing while we were waiting and somehow your name came up. I think I said I was meeting you the next day. 'Ah, that Richard Demarco,' said the Italian-Scot proprietor from behind the counter. 'Sure he's only a wee fish and chip man like myself – except he's selling something else.' And indeed, 'selling something else' is what you have always done. In 2001 you celebrated your pan-European cultural heritage by becoming Director of the Demarco European Arts Foundation, and you have done immense work to bring Europe to Edinburgh. At ninety I propose a new title: 'Old Ricky, Ambassador Extraordinaire to Auld Reekie!'

Love, Max

ACTORS

Rachel Roberts: born September 20, 1927, died November 26, 1980. Rachel was in two iconic films of the 1960s: *Saturday Night and Sunday Morning* and *This Sporting Life*. She won Baftas for both and was nominated for an Academy Award for best actress for *This Sporting Life*. Other notable film appearances include *Murder on the Orient Express, Picnic at Hanging Rock* and *Yanks*. But she was also a distinguished stage actress, winning a Tony award for *Chemin de Fer* and *The Visit*, and a Drama Desk award two years later for *Habeas Corpus*. In 1960 she starred in *Platonov* at the Royal Court with Rex Harrison. A year later they married in Italy. The marriage was volcanic: both drank excessively and they fought publicly. It was well known that Rachel was a serious alcoholic.

November 26, 2019

Dear Rachel,

I don't know how many people before me were invited to direct *The End of Me Old Cigar* by John Osborne, but I imagine it must have been a good many. The play came with Jill Bennett, Osborne's current wife, already attached, and there was a huge part for Regine, who was the madame of a prosperous Home Counties brothel that recruited fragrant upmarket Kensington wives.

If I had been more experienced, or perhaps I mean wiser, I would probably have turned the play down, for it was a trundling old turkey, garlanded with huge speeches about sex and Regine's misandrist plot to overthrow and humiliate male hierarchy. However, John Osborne's reputation, both as a playwright and as a maverick, made it easy to assemble a stellar cast that included Keith Barron, who had a considerable television pedigree; Sheila Ballantine, who had worked at the RSC; and a young Neil Johnston, whose work with Nancy Meckler and the Freehold company I had long admired. There was also a very attractive but unknown actress called Joanna Lumley, whose cut-glass Home Counties accent sounded totally appropriate.

As I remember, a considerable amount of drama happened before we even started rehearsal. You were living in New York and nobody met you at Heathrow. That was the first mistake. (My then-wife, Carole Hayman, suggests that we picked you up in the Joint Stock van, but I don't remember that.) The Greenwich Theatre had booked you into a pleasant family hotel in Blackheath, quite close to the theatre. That was the second mistake. You took great offence at such undignified treatment and checked into the Dorchester, at the same time telling your agent that there was no way you were going to go ahead with any play in 'fucking Greenwich'. John Osborne and Jill Bennett were furious, but I was able, at one day's notice, to secure the services of another leading actress. However, she lived in Hertfordshire and only consented to play the part if she could have a car to pick her up and take her home each day. This remained the only point that had to be resolved.

At about 11pm on the Saturday before rehearsals were due to start on the Monday the phone rang in our single-room flat in South Villas, Camden. Somewhat incoherently you told me how sorry you were that we would not after all have a chance to meet, and you suggested that Carole and I should come over to the Dorchester straight away for a drink. I was already in bed, exhausted by events, but we dressed hastily and drove to the Dorchester.

The doorman was not enthusiastic about finding a parking space for two hippies in a battered van. However, we got in and were waiting in the lobby when you stepped out of the lift with a respectable gentleman carrying a large Gladstone bag. We had three or four drinks and got on very well. You and Carole took to each other immediately, as I recall. I didn't drink much in those days, and at 1.30am it was way past my bedtime. That was when you announced that you had changed your mind and wished to do *The End of Me Old Cigar* after all. The gentleman who had stepped out of the lift with you was your doctor, and he would testify that the combination of jet lag and the medication you were on had made you temporarily incapable of making a rational decision. Also, the contract that you had already agreed was legal and binding, and if the Greenwich Theatre did not honour it your lawyers would sue them for their entire grant income for the next ten years. I don't remember the conversation after that, but in the van heading back to South Villas Carole said, 'Of course you must have her. If you don't you'll regret it all your life.'

Next day I phoned the agent of the other actress to say that the request for the car was out of the question and regretfully we would have to move on. John Osborne and Jill Bennett were far from reconciled to the situation, but John pragmatically accepted that this was the only possible way forward.

By some serendipitous event, the reading took place at the London Welsh Centre in Gray's Inn Road. You were pleased at that, and told me that your hometown rugby club, Llanelli, regularly trounced London Welsh. The reading itself was pretty spectacular. You were wearing a dazzling white fur coat. Once you had identified Neil as the actor playing your lover, you spread the fur coat on the grotty floor of the rehearsal room, pulled Neil down beside you and flirted outrageously throughout the reading. (I think Neil was a bit puzzled but had no objections to being flirted with by a star.) But you were not unfocused. You attacked the script with huge energy and commitment. It was clear that you were thoroughly prepared. It was a performance like a rough diamond, an uncut stone that glittered with the promise of future wealth. There was a moment when your character sang four lines from an Italian opera. At this point you rose to your feet, using Neil as a leaning post, and sang the aria with total control and in perfect Italian. You told me later that you had been taking singing lessons in New York for two months.

After the reading even Jill Bennett was won over and was markedly less glacial. John Osborne himself grinned at me and simply said, 'Good luck,' as he left. But in fact

I remember rehearsals as very purposeful and pleasant. You had just three responses to my proffered notes. Occasionally: 'That's good, Max. I'll try that.' Sometimes: 'I could have done it like that but it's too late now. I'm doin' somethin' else there.' Or, most often: 'No, Max, that's bollocks. I'm not doin' that.' But all this was offered without any rancour or disdain. And I was quite happy to have my notes assessed so rigorously. You took responsibility for your performance in the manner to which leading actors of your generation were accustomed. That was why Bill Gaskill was so nostalgic about working with Maggie Smith, and often despaired of younger actors. I recall him challenging an actress in rehearsal of *A Mad World, My Masters* with: 'But is that really what you intend to do in performance?'

There was only one alcoholic interlude that I remember. It started in the down-at-heel pub on the Churchill Estate, Pimlico, where we were rehearsing. You bought drinks for the company. You wouldn't let any of us buy a drink, and then on the third round you marched up to the bar, turned to address the entire pub and shouted, 'All right, everybody, the next round is on Rex. What'll you have?' I don't know the terms of your divorce settlement with Rex Harrison, but you told me it was astronomical. After another round I made my excuses and left, but you took the cast to several other watering holes before ending up at the Dorchester. Anticipating how the evening might end, you were given a rehearsal time of 12 for the following day, but somehow the message did not get through and you arrived promptly at 10am – frisky and ready to work.

Other members of the cast were late and rather the worse for wear.

One Saturday morning the parish hall that we had been using for rehearsal was booked for a jumble sale and we had to find an alternative rehearsal space. We borrowed the stage at the Royal Court for the morning and you were more than delighted to revisit that hallowed space where you and Rex Harrison had triumphed in *Platonov*. We had a good morning's work but at lunchtime you beckoned me onstage. You led me up the stairs past the stage door and I saw that you had a key in your hand with a pink ribbon tied to a large wooden name tag. You continued up the stairs and stopped outside the No 1 dressing room. I was alarmed, fearing that the rightful occupant might have already arrived for the matinee. But as you threw the door open I saw that it was unoccupied. You stepped back and said, 'My God, it's still there!' and pointed towards a battered green sofa as if it were a relic of the True Cross. 'Rex had me on that sofa. The dirty bastard got me up here to go over his lines with him and he had me on that sofa. Ooh, it was lovely.'

Osborne attended rehearsal only very occasionally but he gave me a wonderful first-night present: a beautifully illustrated coffee-table book about the history of music hall. I wish I knew where it was today. There were two other spin-offs from the production. You and Jill Bennett became firm chums and spent a lot of time together when you both lived in LA. Also *The End of Me Old Cigar* seemed to give you back an appetite for the theatre, and I think it was the following year that you won a Tony for your performances in *The Visit* and *Chemin de Fer* on Broadway.

Carole Hayman was right. I wouldn't have missed you for anything. You were Top Talent. I'm so glad I met you, Rachel Roberts.

Love,

Max

Gary Oldman came from a working-class background and had some early, and considerable, encouragement. He had played several big roles at the Glasgow Citizens and had also played in a West End run of *Summit Conference*, by Robert David Macdonald. He won two awards, from *Time Out* and *Drama*, for his performance as Scopey in *The Pope's Wedding*. His film career has been extraordinarily successful and he has won many other awards, culminating in an Oscar for his performance as Winston Churchill in *The Darkest Hour*.

April 4, 2018

Dear Gary,

We haven't met for a while, so first of all let me say how delighted I was at your brilliant and well-deserved Oscar triumph. I was also touched and tickled a week later to get a clipping of an interview with *The Hollywood Reporter* in which you showed the reporter your film script, covered with 'actions' or intentions. This was the method we used when we worked together on *The Pope's Wedding*, *Rat in the Skull* and *Serious Money*.

I don't remember if we met at Westcliff-on-Sea. I remember driving down to see Chris Dunham's excellent production of *Saved* but I don't remember if we met afterwards. Did we have fish and chips in Westcliff, or am I making that up? At the time I was planning a season of Edward Bond plays that would pair *Saved* with his first play, *The Pope's Wedding*, which had previously only had a solitary Sunday-night performance at the Royal Court.

I thought your performance in *Saved* was confident and strong but, to be candid, I didn't fully appreciate your great emotional range or the scope of your transformative skills until we worked together. At this distance, my clearest recollection of Westcliff is that there were approximately 40 people in the audience at the beginning of the evening and about half that number at the end. I admired Chris Dunham's bottle and bravery as much as I did his directing skills. It was an example of commitment and integrity which I knew I would do well to emulate at the Royal Court.

Like *Next Time I'll Sing to You*, by James Saunders, *The Pope's Wedding* is a strange story of the hermit of Great Canfield, who chose to live a solitary life in a shed at the bottom of somebody's garden. Together with Tony Rohr, who played the hermit, we drove down to deepest Essex to inspect the shed. You played Scopey, a village lad whose girlfriend, Pam, regularly supplied provisions to the old man. Lesley Manville played Pam. She had already made her Royal Court debut as a lively guinea pig in a play that had been part of a Young Writers Festival Upstairs. There was a moment in rehearsal when Lesley was finding it difficult to open the door to the shed while holding the shopping basket full of apples and tins of evaporated milk. You solved the problem by saying, 'Look, I can help here,' and holding the basket for her. At that moment I perceived, by the tender look between you both, that you were falling in love. And indeed, you later married. It was also the beginning of my yet-to-be-realised plan to write a coffee-table book of Royal Court romances. This would include Joan Plowright and Lawrence Olivier, Harley Granville Barker and Lillah McCarthy, Rex Harrison and Rachel Roberts, Danny Boyle and Gail Stephens, Adrian Dunbar and Anna Nygh. It is totally fitting that Lesley was nominated for an Oscar in the same year as you, and that you attended the ceremony together.

When I was in Edinburgh at the Traverse I spent much time and thought consulting *Spotlight* in the search for actors I might entice up to Edinburgh. Initially the definitions in *Spotlight* of 'leading actor', 'character actor' meant little to me. One afternoon a senior Scottish actor, Callum Mill, explained to me that if you were planning a season which included a production of, say, *Hamlet*, you would need younger leading actors for Hamlet and Ophelia, a leading actor and a leading actress for Claudius and Gertrude, a character actor for Polonius, and possibly two younger character actors for Rosencrantz and Guildenstern. Thus equipped, you had a core company that could undertake most classics.

The qualities required for leading actors and leading actresses are elusive and can't readily be taught at drama school. You need charm and charisma. And, above all, a leading player requires a certain magnetism that pulls the audience towards their particular character's dilemma and holds them there unremittingly. I have spent considerable time in my career endeavouring to turn younger character actors into leading actors – not always successfully. I struck lucky with you and with Lesley Manville. You filled the stage with your relationship and made the leap to younger leading actors seem effortless, and now you have both seamlessly become major leading actors.

The next play we did together was *Rat in the Skull* by Ron Hutchinson. This play, too, told an unexpected story. It was set in a cell at Paddington Green Police Station, where a Republican prisoner was being interrogated by a visiting RUC inspector (played by Brian Cox) about further possible crimes committed in Ireland. Phil Jackson played a senior Metropolitan Police officer detailed to supervise the interrogation, and you were a rookie constable, detailed to guard the prisoner. The play unexpectedly detoured into an account of the Troubles, interpreted largely from the perspective of the visiting RUC inspector. The general expectation was that the play would be sympathetic to, or at least understanding of, the Republican cause, but instead embraced a royalist perspective.

Even though it was only a four-hander, the cash-strapped Royal Court required extra funding to proceed with the production, and we had applied to the Greater London Council. A meeting was arranged and the Royal Court's general manager, Graham Cowley, and I attended it in the GLC's Southbank redoubt. We were kept waiting for an hour and a half before a functionary finally appeared. Then things went remarkably quickly: 'Royal Court, Irish play. The leader [Ken Livingstone] is particularly enthusiastic about this application. I think you can rely on a sum of £18,000.' The play continues to be revived and is now generally seen as a significant contribution to the ongoing debate about Ireland that the theatre has hosted.

For reasons I don't recall, you were unavailable and missed out on the trip to New York when the play formed the third instalment of our exchange with the Public Theater. *The New York Times* critic Frank Rich approved, calling *Rat in the Skull* 'a raw descent into the murderous morass of Northern Ireland'. I think the American public were confused both by the Northern Irish accents and by an Ulster Protestant as the central figure. However, Joe Papp really liked it and that was always the most significant approval required at the Public Theater.

You also missed a great outing organised by Phil Jackson to hear Van Morrison play at the Apollo. (There is a musical detour in this letter. Stop reading for a moment and play Van Morrison's 'Cleaning Windows'.) Like you and Andrea, Van came from a working-class background, and the song celebrates a time when he was 'playing saxophone at the weekends' with a show band while earning a living by working with a window-cleaning gang. Phil had become acquainted with Van during the making of the Paul McCartney film *Give My Regards to Broad Street.* After the concert Van's manager, who had arranged the tickets, told us that Van would like to meet us at the Central Cafe, just around the block. Van had some blondes, he added. I assumed they were some kind of fashionable amphetamines, but the blondes turned out to be… well, two blondes. One was a travel agent from Toronto and one a hairdresser from Long Island who had been accumulated on Van's tour. Van ignored them and they ignored us completely. So conversation was hard going until Van suddenly asked forcefully and earnestly whether we thought Rimbaud was a better poet than Verlaine. None of us had any great experience in French versification, but I had done a year of subsidiary French in the Lower VI, 25 years earlier, and, drawing a bow at a venture, said tentatively that Rimbaud was possibly the greater poet but that Verlaine was perhaps the greater technician. This was undoubtedly nonsense, but it seemed to keep the great man happy.

When we started work on *Serious Money* in September 1986, your film career was already beginning to take off. We started with two weeks' workshop/research, when we did our best to penetrate the arcane world of London's financial markets. Linda Bassett and Meera Syal got jobs as runners on the floor of LIFFE, the London International Financial Futures Exchange. Their new colleagues were amazed and concerned at how little money they earned. We met stockbrokers, traders on the Metal Exchange and on the Baltic Exchange, and hung out with Terry and Tracey, two traders from the floor of LIFFE, who insisted on buying us champagne in the Greenhouse Champagne Bar every evening. The two tribes peered at each other with amused curiosity. Clearly they thought we had taken some absurd life decisions, but on the other hand we were working with Ian Dury, who was writing songs for the show, and he had iconic status with the Essex boys and girls on the trading floor of LIFFE. When Ian visited Linda and Meera the stunned traders stopped trading. He was promptly banned from the trading floor. LIFFE was tolerant about all kinds of behaviour but the one unforgivable sin was to stop making money.

One evening in the Greenhouse Bar, Terry said he wouldn't be able to meet us on Friday as he had to go to Toronto to secure some futures in pork bellies. By an extraordinary coincidence you had to fly to Toronto to start work on a film that overlapped with the workshop by one day, and you were both on the same flight. You agreed to meet for a drink en route but Terry spotted a problem. He said, 'I'm flying business class, but don't worry, I'll come back and find you.' And you said, 'I'm flying first class, but don't worry, I'll come back and find you.' No wonder they were confused about our status.

Caryl's script was an extraordinary achievement. It conveyed disapproval of the naked greed of the financial world, while at the same time the bouncing verse in which it was written captured the piratical excitement and energy. The play was a big success and ran for a year in the West End after its run at the Royal Court.

One image particularly stays in the mind. In the summer Shearson Lehman had bought out a whole performance for their staff and clients. It was a hot night and the doors of the theatre lobby leading to Sloane Square were left open to get some air circulating. Unfortunately a gas main was being replaced in Sloane Square and the square was part-closed to traffic while men with drills, naked to the waist, excavated a series of trenches. In the interval I apologised for the unbearable noise to our contact at Shearson Lehman. 'Don't worry, mate,' he said.

'I'll sort it.' He opened two bottles of champagne and placed them on a large tray on the box-office counter, together with a dozen champagne flutes. With aplomb he swept into Sloane Square, approaching each of the men with an irresistible deal: 'No more drilling and as much champagne as you want.' Within minutes complete peace had returned. The men sat on the road with their feet dangling in the trenches, quaffing champagne. They looked like the sweaty and muscular workmen depicted in Rubens's great painting *The Raising of the Cross*.

Of course I rejoice in your cinematic triumphs, but I hope you will not altogether reject the theatre, the scene of your early victories.

Best wishes,

Love, Max

Billy Hinchliff is 18 and currently applying to various drama schools, having completed a year-long foundation course at Guildhall. He has been offered a place at the Royal Welsh Drama College for the year 2019/20 but is currently involved in the National Youth Theatre's Summer Repertory which would overlap with the beginning of the drama-school year. After much deliberation he has decided to postpone drama school and commit to the NYT season.

Billy comes from Sheffield and often stays with his aunt in London. She is a neighbour and friend of my sister-in-law and they walk their dogs together. Through her I offered to help Billy with his audition pieces when he began the arduous round of drama-school auditions. Together we worked on scenes from *Hamlet*, *Henry IV Part One*, *Measure for Measure*, *Kes* and *Antigone*.

What I didn't know at the start was that Billy has considerable talent, and given a modicum of luck – which any actor needs – he should go far. What he doesn't know is that working with him is the only directing work I have done in the past two years and has not only been extremely pleasurable but has provided very necessary therapy. Billy is enjoying his time at the NYT, working with kids who left school at 13 and also with old Etonians.

Billy saved up for drama school by working at Wilko's in Sheffield from 5pm to 10pm. Work involves filling different crates in the basement, lugging the crates to the lift, going up to the shop floor and filling the shelves. After work he has a quick drink with a friend before catching the last bus, the 120, home. While Billy was saving for drama school, his friend was saving to expand his collection of exotic pets. He has a parrot, a macaw, two Staffy pups, and his next acquisition will be a monkey. Shelf-stackers have dreams.

March 17, 2019

Dear Billy,

I think you are probably taking the best decision in turning down drama school for the present and persisting with the NYT repertory. I understand you are to be Lysander in *A Midsummer Night's Dream*, so congratulations on that and I look forward to seeing it. If it goes well and you receive much praise and attention I hope you will resist the temptation to bypass drama school and plunge into the profession straight away. At drama school you will befriend colleagues whose journey through the profession will parallel your own and, most importantly, you will absorb a methodology which you can adapt and make your own. You will have recourse to this if you play Romeo but can't abide Juliet, or if you come across a director who is little help and you are then thrown back on your own resources.

In our most recent session we worked on a scene from *Antigone*. I had been rather apprehensive about working on a Greek play. I know the ground-breaking excellence of Greek tragedy, but I find them very hard to relate to and I can't imagine myself electing to direct one – all those grand emotions and bizarrely extreme situations (sleeping with your mum, killing your own kids). I realise this is a lack of imagination on my part, but I was very happy with the work we did in the 90 minutes we had together.

You were working on the scene where Harmon warns his father, Creon, that the cruelty and extreme measures Creon has taken against Antigone have provoked serious and dangerous opposition from the people. I thought you made real progress when you began to think of Creon just as a father and to imagine the complexities of advising, warning, unnerving and even threatening your dad. All these are actions, you will note. Was Harmon closer to his dad than to his mum? Did Creon discipline Harmon when he was naughty? Does Harmon admire Creon as king? Is Harmon apprehensive now about giving him advice that he may well take as criticism? Might Creon strike Harmon if he gets angry? All father-son relationships are particular, dense and complex. Go further with this work. Does Creon confide in Harmon? If Creon had a secret, would he tell Harmon? Make the relationship close and you will find some of the things you have to say to your dad in the scene difficult to get to, which will add texture to the scene. Finally, is revolution in the air? Is there a sense that if Creon persists with his cruelty there could be an insurrection? If there was, what would Harmon do? Would he fight to protect his dad, or would he side with the revolutionaries? These thoughts and questions will help to make the material more familiar.

I don't think familiarity will breed contempt, but it could lead to a kind of carelessness. The language is not colloquial or demotic. It was crafted by Sophocles in 442 BC, doubtless scraping with his stylus by candlelight, and then it has been reforged by Seamus Heaney, who I heard described on television last night as 'a master craftsman of language'. So phrasing, articulation, breathing – and above all observing the punctuation – will be crucial to the delivery. Remember that punctuation is a direction the writer bequeaths to the actor, so don't you go turning commas into full stops. And when you work at the RSC, as one day you surely will, they will teach you that it is always the verb and never the pronoun that you must colour in a sentence.

But let's have a brief recap about approaching a text and the use of actions. Most importantly it leads actors to elucidate what they want and the tactics they take to achieve that. So actioning the text is when we describe the intention of a line with a transitive verb. In this case Max 'teaches' Billy. And for the first rehearsal or two I would get the actor to articulate the action before saying the line.

A Midsummer Night's Dream is hard to relate to as well, because it is as formally structured as a woodcut, and because the emotions of the characters are often controlled by magic. Does Lysander really hate Hermia in the middle of the play? You could adapt an exercise of Stanislavski's here – emotional recall. I know you have just broken up with your girlfriend, because she was in Sheffield and you were in London and absence did not make the hearts grow fonder. Understandably the breakup made you sad and miserable, but let's say it made you angry instead, and that Hermia/your girlfriend had gone off with that bloke you least liked in school. Pick a card at random from a pack of playing cards. Let's say it's a six. Now play the scene six-out-of-ten angry and pissed off with Hermia. Choosing the card at random liberates you from having to think how angry you are. Your only task is to depict it accurately. Having done that, now select an eight from the pack and see how that changes the scene. So far the emotions have been determined at random. Only now choose the card you think is most appropriate – probably that is the right level of anger – and see what that does to the scene!

Very best wishes and I look forward to our next session.

As ever,

Max

Montgomery Clift, born October 17, 1920, Omaha, Nebraska. Died July 23, 1966, New York. An American motion-picture actor noted for the emotional depth and sense of vulnerability he brought to his roles. Along with Marlon Brando and James Dean, he helped delineate a new paradigm for American cinematic heroes. His films include *Red River, A Place in the Sun* and *From Here to Eternity* – for which he won an Academy Award.

July 2, 2020

Dear Monty,

I wish I had been a little older when we met and that I had understood more about the theatre and how it worked. I would have been fascinated to talk to you about the early days of the Studio, when you were directed by Lee Strasberg and Elia Kazan and worked with James Dean and Marlon Brando. I knew that in 1956 you had been in a severe and damaging car crash, but I had not fully understood that you had been in an equally traumatic crash of a very different kind immediately before we met.

You had been on location in Munich, filming *Freud*, directed by John Huston, and you had had a spectacular and damaging falling-out with him. The problems had begun with Jean-Paul Sartre's impossibly verbose script, which in its initial version ran to 1,600 pages and would have lasted ten hours on film. Endless rewrites followed, edited by Huston himself and the producer, Wolfgang Reinhardt. Sartre later wished to have his name taken off the credits.

My father, a prominent psychiatrist, had been engaged as an adviser, but he had also become involved with the rewrites and later his role morphed into acting as your counsellor, friend, supporter and psychiatrist, as you began to have a fully fledged nervous breakdown. Huston had a notoriously low tolerance for vulnerability, and in addition he was shocked and horrified, just as shooting started, to discover that you were homosexual. Under the circumstances it was not surprising that you had difficulty remembering the lines.

On the day before I arrived in Munich to visit my dad, Huston had insisted on 29 takes of a particular shot, no longer with the expectation of obtaining a better take, but with a determination to humiliate you. Two days after Daddy and I left Munich to go back to London, you had a major confrontation with Huston. It was later vividly recalled by Wolfgang Reinhardt. 'I was sitting in my office when someone rushed in and said, "You must come at once." I could hear high-pitched noises coming from Monty's dressing room. What I saw as I peered through the door chilled me. The mirror was broken, every chair smashed, the couch torn apart, broken glass all over the place. In the middle of it all stood John Huston. "I taught that little bastard a lesson," Huston said. "I had him trembling in a corner. Maybe he'll start to remember his lines a little better now." He finished with a stream of four-letter words.'

You must have found it a far cry from Elia Kazan, who believed in a deeply personal relationship with his actors: 'To encourage real acting you have to understand the actors' problems and hang-ups,' Kazan once wrote.

After shooting in Munich had finished you lingered for a few days in a state of post-traumatic shock, and it was then that you started drinking heavily. In his biography of you, Robert La Guardia writes, 'The fatigue turned into something deep and terrifying that attacked the whole psyche.' Doris Langley Moore, the vastly experienced costume designer, who had championed you in the civil war with Huston, heard of your distressed state and invited you to London to stay in her house in Regent's Park. However, a toxic mixture of alcohol and amphetamines made it impossible for you to sleep, and after a week of keeping her whole household awake Doris tactfully suggested you might be better off in a hotel. You moved into the Savoy, but your heavy drinking continued. Your 'food-throwing episodes in public' also continued, on this occasion in the Savoy Grill. Robert La Guardia suggested, 'Monty had a need to relive his staid childhood, this time as an unmitigated brat.'

It was from the Savoy that my father picked you up one Friday night to spend a long weekend at our home in the leafy suburbs of Woldingham, Surrey. On Saturday my parents decided to take you and the whole family out to lunch. Perhaps today the Good Companions in Upper Warlingham is a bistro pub, but in those days it was simply a pub that served food, and not very posh food at that. My parents were not gourmets and my father often proclaimed that he did not care for 'messed-about food'. His restaurant of choice in London was Verreys in Regent Street, which had been Charles Dickens' favourite eating place, and its stolid menu and decor had not changed much in the intervening century.

You were in exuberant mood at the Good Companions and jumped to your feet at one point, flourishing your napkin in one hand and a chicken leg in the other. 'I know you,' you declared. 'You're rubber chicken. We've met on many occasions.' My mother had no great experience of Hollywood stars, but she had a keen nose for bad table manners. 'Monty, put the chicken back on your plate. Sit down and put your napkin on your lap,' she snapped. 'And for goodness' sake sit up straight,' she added. You too had a mother who was a stickler for etiquette and you obeyed with alacrity.

We had no spare room and the sleeping arrangements were improvised. You took my bedroom on the ground floor, along the corridor from my parents' room, and I moved upstairs to share a room with my younger brothers, Jonathan and Nigel.

Next morning was a clear, bright December day and as I came downstairs for breakfast I realised I needed a sweater. I walked along the corridor to my own room and stopped outside the door, wondering if I should knock. The door was not properly closed and I could hear voices. Carefully I eased the door slightly wider, and I could see you sitting in your pyjamas on the edge of my bed. You were sobbing openly and loudly. My father was sitting diagonally opposite you in the armchair, with his dressing gown on and his back to the door. He was talking quietly.

I realised that under the circumstances a sweater was no longer a priority and retreated to the kitchen for breakfast.

It is a tribute both to your transformative acting skills and to my father's healing powers that you both arrived 20 minutes later, dressed, shaved and with no visible signs of distress. In the course of the weekend your charm conquered both the female members of the household: my mother and my 19-year-old sister, Scylla. You bonded particularly with my lively and super-intelligent youngest brother, Nigel. The whole family petitioned for a return visit. This didn't happen and you returned to New York.

However, my father's involvement in your story continued. *Freud* had gone enormously over budget and Universal International attempted to recoup their losses by suing the insurance company for over half a million dollars. In the meantime they declined to pay the balance of your fee. Essential to their claim was that you had a chronic medical condition and your inability to remember lines was the principal cause of delays. This claim in turn depended on the testimony of various doctors to verify that you were in a state of near collapse. They were, however, unconvincing at the tribunal as they admitted that most of their information had in fact come from Universal's executives themselves. La Guardia comments, 'The doctor Universal really counted on, Dr David Stafford-Clark, refused to "go along".' In his deposition he suggested that Monty had been 'harassed by the executives'. Universal had to settle out of court and the balance of your fee was paid. My father comes out of the story very well and it is timely to return his compliment*: 'I don't know exactly what you did as a psychiatrist but I do know that you did it extremely well.'

In 1962 I had little idea that I was on the threshold of a life in the theatre myself, and I did not pause to consider why the toxic mixture of talent, fame, money and alcohol made such a poisonous and addictive cocktail for so many great actors and musicians. Nor did I fully realise that you were one of the great actors of your generation. La Guardia writes, 'Montgomery Clift was and still is one of the most important influences on contemporary motion picture acting... the intensity and truth of Al Pacino, Robert De Niro or Jack Nicholson can be traced back to the strivings of Monty Clift.'

But I did sense that you had an extraordinary quality of openness and that you retained the fundamental decency and freshness of a Quaker-reared country lad from Nebraska even as you were fighting with your debilitating demons. Later, when I saw *From Here to Eternity*, I also recognised the perverse stubbornness and self-destructive integrity you brought so vividly to the role of Prewitt, and I understood for the first time that a great actor has to bring his own vulnerability, together with his talent, to the stage. Actors are regularly required to haul up performances from a dark place within themselves. It is necessary to bring emotions to the surface and an actor requires strong support to balance the required vulnerability.

I subsequently worked at different times with two young actresses who later both committed suicide. If they had

---

* See page 46

instead been working as primary-school teachers I wonder if they would both be still alive. Many fine, talented actors may appear to be doing well: a show in Manchester, a play at the Globe, a couple of voice-overs even, then a play at the Park. But in fact they are probably barely earning £18,000 a year. The attrition rate grows as responsibilities arrive: marriage, a mortgage, children. It's tough, and as Timberlake Wertenbaker feelingly wrote in *Our Country's Good*, 'You have to be brave to be an actor.' The nerves don't go away and the artistic fulfilment is as unreliable as the finances. Actors themselves recognise this all too well, and Alan Rickman and Ian McKellen are two examples of successful and well-rewarded actors who have been extraordinarily generous and supportive to less-fortunate colleagues.

You yourself were a brave actor, and you certainly experienced both triumph and disaster. Your own personal demons have been well documented over the decades. Indeed your death has been described as 'the longest suicide note in history'.

In his copy of *Montgomery Clift* by Robert La Guardia my father has written a short poem. It is dated 1977, 11 years after your death.

These tales of wanton battles long ago
Approach the truth, then back away.
While we who fought recalling what we know,
Remember what we said – and would not say.

Best wishes,
Max

Archie Redford is a third-year student at the Royal Welsh College of Music and Drama in Cardiff. I worked on his audition pieces with him when he applied to the college three years ago.

August 2, 2020

Dear Archie,

Thank you for your letter and I'm delighted to hear that you are undertaking a verbatim project at the Royal Welsh College. I think you have started well and the subject you have chosen – 'The Effects of Covid-19 on the Welsh Tourist Industry' – is sufficiently wide-ranging that it leaves you with a lot to explore. Of course you must read and prepare as widely as possible, but funnily enough ignorance can also be an advantage, as the script will record your learning curve through the process.

The first job for each of the actors in your group will be to find a character that interests them who they would like to play. They can then follow up any group meetings with individual meetings with the person concerned. I've often found it useful to locate a character who stands somewhat outside the group but who can act as an informed and hopefully impartial guide and interpreter of events. In *The Permanent Way* it was the British Transport

Police Superintendent who conducted the investigation into the Paddington crash. In *Talking to Terrorists* it was Edward, a psychiatrist, who provided an analysis of how a young idealist may become a terrorist, and in *Crouch, Touch, Pause, Engage* Neil Kinnock was our trusty guide to the rise and fall of the Welsh industrial base, and a knowledgeable and entertaining companion at the rugby matches we attended.

Crouch, Touch, Pause, Engage is probably the most complex verbatim play with which I have been involved and certainly one of the most rewarding. It contained two distinct storylines: one involving the Welsh rugby star Gareth Thomas coming out to his teammates, and the other concerning a group of young people at Bridgend College who were themselves victims of third-generation unemployment, which had led to a great deal of self-harming and to a shocking wave of teenage suicides, which was at the time misleadingly reported in the red-top newspapers as a mysterious satanic cult.

The point again is that though you must start with a general purpose you must be ready to absorb the surprises and contradictions you encounter on the way. One small example would be the meeting Robin Soans and I had with Norman Tebbit while working on *Talking to Terrorists*. Correct liberal-left opinion had him as an ogre. *Spitting Image* depicted him as a crash-helmeted Nazi biker. So it was a bouleversement to find him a genial and helpful host who dispensed excellent chocolate biscuits and some very good jokes about Mrs Thatcher. His political opinions were outrageously and unrepentantly right-wing, but to witness at first hand the lifelong injuries he and his wife had suffered as a result of the Brighton bomb prompted a certain admiration for his stoicism and determination.

During the course of our research we also met Patrick Magee, the IRA bombmaker who had planted the bomb in the Grand Hotel in Brighton. I had been prepared to acknowledge his commitment, but I found myself chilled and shocked by his advocacy of the Armalite and the bomb.

Another character we met during the *Talking to Terrorists* workshop who took me by surprise was the colonel. By this point we had met various extraordinary revolutionary figures from Chechnya, Palestine, Northern Ireland and Uganda, and I seriously underestimated the impact that this British army officer would make on us all. To start with my idea of a colonel was probably stuck somewhere in 1935 with the image of a pipe-smoking, tweedy, upper-class gent. But Colonel Iron was dapper, cool and immaculately dressed in a Thomas Pink shirt. He was good-looking and much younger than I had anticipated. The first thing he did was to camouflage himself and become invisible within the group. Within 20 minutes he had taken off his smart blazer, loosened his tie and slouched over the table. Anybody entering the room at that point would almost certainly have taken him for one of the actors. The session with him that afternoon was riveting as he talked about his two tours of duty in South Armagh, and of how if he had been born in Crossmaglen he too would in all probability have become a terrorist. Getting into the minds of the men who wanted to kill him was, he explained, crucial to his survival. He was, in all senses of the word, very clever – the army had given him a scholarship to Cambridge, where of course he got a first.

The essence of verbatim is that you are talking to people who have actually lived the story, and their eloquence and authenticity is captured in their own words. In Caryl Churchill's play *Light Shining in Buckinghamshire* she evokes the animated excitement of people taking hold of their own lives and their gradual betrayal as those who led them realised that freedom could not be had without property being destroyed. Her exploration of this world where Christ's second coming is expected imminently is massively and painstakingly thorough, but it is completed by an extraordinary verbatim scene taken down by secretaries when they recorded the vigorous and heated debate in a church in Putney between the various factions of the victorious Parliamentary army in 1647. Cromwell has talked of the 'difficulties' of extending the franchise to men who had no property and who therefore, in his view, held no stake in the country. While Colonel Rainsborough forcefully argued that any common soldier who had risked their lives had fully demonstrated their commitment and stake in their country. Here is a brief and condensed extract, with one or two possible actions suggested.

(Actions in brackets)

CROMWELL: [stalls] These things you have offered they are new to us. It is the first time we have had a view of them. (sobers) Truly they do contain very great alterations of the very government of the Kingdom. (humours) If we would leap out of one condition into another I don't suppose there would be much dispute. (cautions) We must consider the ways and means; (grounds) whether the people are prepared to go along with it and (sobers) whether the great difficulties in our way are likely to be overcome.

RAINSBOROUGH: (mocks) Truly I think Parliament were very indiscreet to engage with the King if they did not consider first that they should go through difficulties; (ridicules) I think there was no man who entered into the war that did not engage to go through difficulties. (braces) Truly I think let the difficulties be round you, death before you, and the sea behind you and you are convinced the thing is just, (fires) you are bound in conscience to carry it on.

CROMWELL: (softens) Truly I am glad this gentleman is here. (amuses) We shall enjoy his company longer than I thought we should.

RAINSBOROUGH: (embitters) If I should not be kicked out.

The agenda, but not the language, could be that of a Labour Party Conference with the leadership on the platform (Cromwell) attempting to defuse and dilute some radical Momentum proposal.

It is the language which is so extraordinary, so rich and so articulate, and the arguments on both sides so clear. These are the actual words that were spoken in the Church of St Mary the Virgin, Putney, on October 28, 1647, and hearing them never failed to give me a shiver of excitement.

So, Archie, authenticity is perhaps the single most valuable delivery that verbatim brings, but here I should emphasise the importance of the editing and selection undertaken by your director and writer.

Always remember that you are telling a story even though you are borrowing other people's words to do so. You should certainly give the people you interview an opportunity to read your eventual script, and you must be prepared to respond to any objections they may have. In practice people tend to be upset by what you leave out rather than by what you include. In the text of *The Permanent Way* the chairman of Great North Eastern said, 'Thank Christ it's not our crash!' when he heard a particular accident had been caused by a defective rail rather than a fault with the train itself. But he went on to talk of the 'rehearsals' he put in place in the event of a further accident. It didn't seem relevant and we cut it. But, quite reasonably, he felt aggrieved that his defence had been excluded. David Hare took the point and re-edited the passage.

As we were then, you will be dealing with people whose feelings will be tender, and you must recognise that. You will meet people who have lost loved ones and people whose businesses have gone bust as a result of the pandemic. You should also make a point of meeting people who have profited from it: undertakers, online supermarkets and, as people are unable to travel abroad, self-catering holiday homes in West Wales are becoming booked out.

David Hare has provided a definition that you may

find useful. He talks of plays where he has 'borne witness' to a person or an event, and 'plays of the imagination'. Clearly these are not so rigidly separated as the definition implies. After all, most plays combine an element of both witness and imagination. Verbatim may also act as a guide or corrective to the actors' instinctive reactions to lines. While researching *The Permanent Way* we met a woman whose son had been killed in the Paddington crash. She recounted to us her trip to the morgue to identify the corpse of her son: 'They had put his nose on wrong… it was all sideways. And they had given him a centre parting and he never had a centre parting in his life.'

Any actor looking at the script would take the action the mother is playing to be 'appals' or 'horrifies', but in fact it was much more interesting and much more complicated. She was a woman with a large personality who enjoyed being the focus of the whole group for the afternoon, and the action she played was more like 'amazes' or even 'entertains'. I don't intend to trivialise her very real grief for a moment, but she had become the spokesperson for the group of bereaved parents, and she had in the process also become an accomplished storyteller.

But the categories are not always as clear as that last answer implies. I have told you about the verbatim scene in *Light Shining in Buckinghamshire* and I believe that Caryl also employed scenes based on verbatim interviews in both *Mad Forest* and *Fen*. Certainly while researching *Bang, Bang, Bang*, Stella's play about human rights researchers working in the Democratic Republic of Congo, we talked to a number of NGO workers, and I expect some of their phrases were embodied in the script. One particularly experienced human rights observer told us of an encounter with an alarming warlord in the jungle. After she had finished her story I set up an improvisation in which she played herself and an actor played the warlord. Then they replayed the events and the shifts in mood which she had outlined. Stella certainly took account of this when writing the scene, though it can hardly be termed 'verbatim'.

You asked which verbatim piece I 'enjoyed' working on most and, to be frank, this is the most difficult question to respond to. I think *Talking to Terrorists* was one of the most revelatory and disturbing plays I have ever worked on and told a most challenging story. But *Mixed Up North* was equally dangerous and we were actively discouraged from continuing. Trish, the social worker in Burnley who started the theatre group in which the young people were involved, feared they would be disturbed and upset by their stories being used. In fact they were delighted that their stories were heard. The Bolton Octagon, who were Out of Joint's partners in the project, were rightly concerned they might have to field allegations of racism as one strand of the stories told to us concerned a group of Asian men clearly grooming a number of underage young women and seducing them with drugs. These stories were important and were clearly true and we persisted. Following the play's run in London various journalists followed up the story and six months later *The Times* printed a series of revelations which ultimately led to a number of prosecutions.

Equally important was *A State Affair*, conceived as a companion piece to a revival of *Rita, Sue and Bob Too*, and focusing on the same estate in which Andrea Dunbar had lived. Twenty years on, it had endured a heroin epidemic and all the contingent problems that gave rise to. We talked to kids, *Big Issue* sellers, police and bail-hostel wardens. Again the material was shocking and the grisly story ended with a young man finding that a vein in his foot was the only undamaged vein into which he could shoot up.

By a circuitous route we had befriended the Lord Chancellor's Wife, Lady Irvine, who had been a social worker, and we staged a site-specific performance in the Lord Chancellor's flat in one of the towers of the Palace of Westminster. You asked about 'enjoyable': it was certainly among the most enjoyable and unexpected pleasures ever to watch the performance with my back to one of the mullioned windows of the tower and with tourist boats passing on the river a hundred feet below. Every member of the audience was a lord and they listened attentively until one of them whispered, 'Division,' at which point every one of them rose and, to a man, our audience disappeared.

Crouch, Touch, Pause, Engage gave me much pleasure too. Each of the actors played the central character, Gareth Thomas; the set was a rugby changing room; and each actor playing Gareth donned a Welsh rugby shirt and was passed the rugby ball. It was a simple device I had stolen from Bill Gaskill's production of *The Ragged-Trousered Philanthropists*, where the autocratic foreman of the group of painters and decorators simply put on a bowler hat. In

Crouch, Touch, Pause Engage the actors were meticulous in the way they passed the ball to each other. After all, if you're playing Gareth Thomas you can't drop it!

It's easy to pinpoint my most frustrating verbatim project too! In September 2015 I spent two weeks working with a company of actors in the premises of a well-set-up amateur theatre group in Stevenage. The initial idea was to explore the reality of life in one of England's post-war new towns and to compare our experiences with the lofty ideals with which the new towns had been founded. But once again we stumbled across a quite different story. We interviewed a young woman whose boyfriend was in prison for drug dealing, and in the course of the two-week workshop discovered that many heavyweight London gangs had shifted their operation into small county towns where the police were less sophisticated and where their presence was unexpected.

During rehearsals of *Pitcairn*, by Richard Bean, I had met Superintendent Rob Viner of the Kent Police, who had led the whole investigation into allegations of paedophilia on Pitcairn Island. As luck would have it, he was now Serious Crime Officer for Kent and Essex, and he readily confirmed what we had found out. He said, 'Yes, gangs here moved to the country. We call it "county lines". I've had to send my plods up to the Met to do a course in detecting heroin routes. Very expensive.' Within six months county lines had become the lead story on *News at Ten*. However, Out of Joint had neither the time nor the resources to take the project further, and after an initial draft by Robin Soans the project was dropped. Also,

Robin's script had included an element of fiction in which an elderly middle-class lady had become sympathetically involved with the central drug dealer. Not only was this reminiscent of *Breaking Bad* but it tore apart the fabric of 'authenticity' Robin had so carefully woven.

With the wisdom of hindsight perhaps we pursued the wrong story. The drug story was exciting, but perhaps the more important story was always where we had first thought it was. We spent one curious afternoon playing bingo with a group of elderly citizens. None of us won but the wonderful Franc Ashman, one of the actors, experienced some rather unpleasant low-level racism. Six months later Stevenage voted overwhelmingly in favour of Brexit. So the story we missed was something like: 'Stevenage: Brexit and Bingo, the bitter story of the disillusion and disappointment of the lower middle class'.

Good luck. The subject you have chosen is engaging and who knows where it may lead you – all over Wales certainly. Be prepared to expand your remit. One of the characteristics of the pandemic is that it has emphasised the independent decision-making that is now possible for the Assemblies of Wales, Scotland and Northern Ireland. Certainly you should interview some senior Welsh political figures.

Best wishes, Max

PLAYWRIGHTS

Andrea Dunbar, born May 22, 1961, died December 20, 1990. Andrea was 19 when I first met her. She had started writing her first play, *The Arbor*, when she was a 16-year-old schoolgirl, prompted by an imaginative English teacher, Mr Cook. Mr Cook sent it to a contact who worked for BBC Leeds, who sent it to a friend in London, Liane Aukin, who sent it to me at the Royal Court. So it had already been through several receptive and encouraging hands before it landed in mine. I subsequently directed three of Andrea's plays and knew her until her death ten years later.

Dear Andrea,

You were always suspicious about middle-class interest in your work. I have never forgotten you saying derisively, 'They'll forget about us by tomorrow.' This has certainly not proved to be the case and there is currently more interest in your work than there has ever been. There was a film, *The Arbor*, by Clio Barnard about your life, a recent radio play about the filming of *Rita, Sue and Bob Too* (*RSB2*), at least two heavyweight academic treatises, and a ludicrously inaccurate book written as if in the first person by you. There has been a proposed American adaptation by Lena Dunham which would transfer the action to rust-belt Connecticut. Most recently I read that members of your family discouraged a play planned for production in Bradford that was to be based on your life, and finally there is talk of another film of *RSB2*.

I am aware that you disapproved of Alan Clarke's film of *Rita, Sue and Bob Too*. You warned me not to see it as you thought 'it were crap'. I learned later that you had been banned from the set as your objections were deemed to have been disruptive. I didn't care for the film much either, though I have seen excellent work by the same director. Your disapproval was largely fuelled by the relentlessly jolly ending in which Rita, Sue and Bob conga off for an endless threesome to the tune of *We're Having a Gangbang*. 'That would never happen,' you said. 'You'd never go back with someone who had let you down.'

I certainly didn't anticipate that your work would continue to be regularly revived, nor that it would accumulate a considerable body of interventionists eager to present their own perspectives on your work. But feminists, Marxists, populists, puritans and apologists of all persuasions should be wary of approaching your work with an agenda. It's as if a straight swig of abrasive, tough, unmediated working-class philosophy and opportunism is too much, too bitter. Certainly there are problems with your work: it has moments of brutality, of sexism and of racism, and sometimes celebrates violence and criminality. You endured much criticism for this from your own community. Your defence was clear: 'That's what's happened. That's how people behave. That's what they said.' Your argument has not been faulted. And in the end your legacy and your achievement is the authenticity of your work.

Some months before I was due to start rehearsal of *RSB2* in a joint production between the Royal Court, Out of Joint and the Bolton Octagon, I was summoned to a meeting at the Royal Court with Vicky Featherstone (Artistic Director) and Lucy Davies (Producer). As the meeting began, Lucy attempted to reassure me that they were simply concerned that the production should be 'right for 2017 and right for the Royal Court'. I never discovered the production they wanted, but they certainly didn't relish the one that transpired, directed by Kate Wasserberg.

I never saw the production. I couldn't bring myself to go to the Royal Court, but I did book two tickets for the Saturday matinee in Oxford. However, my disability means I have to travel with a companion and by this time both Stella and Kitty had had enough. 'Leave it, Dad, just leave it. They don't want you,' said Kitty, with the brutal candour of youth. So I am an unreliable witness, but my instinct is that the performative elements that Kate saw fit to add – disco lighting, mimed and choreographed scene changes to an '80s soundtrack, and some vigorous comic bonking featuring Bob's bobbing bottom – all militated against any serious attempt to depict your tough and gritty world, and inevitably undermined your innate and very real political rage.

Anyway, Vicky Featherstone made a sustained attempt to cancel the Royal Court run. This was accompanied by a press release which laid the blame on 'a conflictual situation' arising from my departure from Out of Joint. But I was booted from Out of Joint at the end of August and Vicky's attempts at cancellation were not made until after she had seen the co-production two and a half months later in Derby. This mess turned yet messier when a Twitter storm accusing her of suppressing free speech forced a retraction of the cancellation. Subsequently all Kate Wasserberg's musical scene changes were removed for the Royal Court run.

But perhaps the clumsiest intervention was made by the *Sunday Times*'s senior drama critic Christopher Hart. His favourite habit was baiting anyone with supposed liberal tendencies. He accused the Royal Court of overzealous political correctness by excluding the character of the violent and abusive Pakistani taxi driver who was your boyfriend. Hart's research did not include reading the text. If he had, he would have discovered that Jousef appears in the second half of *The Arbor* but does not in fact appear at all in *RSB2*. We all have to be careful of appliquéing our own preferences and prejudices onto your work.

Populist, lazy, right-wing thinking would have it that young people in Brafferton Arbor were immoral, and clearly there was not much conventional middle-class morality about. I learned from you that there was a strict moral code of your own, based on unswerving loyalty. Best friends (Sue and Rita) should be unswervingly loyal. Families should be unswervingly loyal to each other. The moral code was there and was well understood by all. The only problem was it was impossible to adhere to, and this was the cause of both friction and violence. Sue and Rita betray each other. Bob betrays Michelle. Brian (the father) attacks both his daughter (Sue) and his wife in public.

He in turn is rejected by the family and in every scene in which he appears in both *The Arbor* and *RSB2* he makes a lonely, defeated exit. In the final scene a kind of armistice is arrived at: Sue defends Rita and acknowledges that Rita's marriage to Bob has created a new loyalty bond that she respects, while Alma (the mother) and Michelle tacitly agree to absolve Sue by placing all the blame on the absent Rita. Thus Michelle preserves her loyalty to Bob and the mother preserves her loyalty to Sue. And Rita shows fealty to Sue by naming her child after her.

Whether you liked it or not, I believe that Alan Clarke's film set a template that determines and conditions audience expectations. The film is often shown on Channel 4 and has accumulated a reputation for sauciness that in turn fans box-office expectations.

I know you were unhappy about how little money you earned. In the last couple of years I believe you would've earned about £40,000 – which has, of course, gone to your three children.

Unforgettably, when you were writing *RSB2* you asked me, 'What can you *do* in theatre?' I was unclear what you were driving at, but I now realise you were asking about sex and how far you could go on stage. If I had realised what you were asking I might have answered more succinctly, along the lines of, 'Sex on stage is exactly like sword-fighting – nobody is killed onstage and nobody fucks either. There is a kind of choreography: one character makes a particular move, which is responded to by a second character, and the illusion of violence or of sexual interplay is created.'

I wish I could tell you that *RSB2* is popular because of its authenticity, or because of the acuity of your writing. To an extent, indeed, this may be true, but the simple truth is that sex on stage or on film sells well. People enjoy watching it. But a transformation often takes place. In real life, watching two people make love may be erotic, it may be embarrassing or it may be offensive, but it is hardly likely to be hilarious. However, on stage it often becomes so, and the same sometimes happens with violence. I remember you watching the furious neighbourhood row in *The Arbor* and commenting wryly, 'It weren't so fucking funny when it were happening, I can tell you.' But this is a slippery slope.

RSB2 is a success on several levels; certainly it is and should be titillating, but it is also successful because it has its roots in the complexities and particularities of a specific society. Without both of these ingredients it can become as simplistic as a saucy seaside postcard. But strangely *RSB2* has become increasingly popular onstage at the same time as the hard-won freedom to depict sex or nudity onstage has met with increased disapproval and self-censorship. If you were to ask me today, 'What can you *do* on stage…?' I would have to answer, 'Probably a lot less than you could in 1981.'

I wish I had been on speaking terms with Kate Wasserberg when she began re-rehearsing *RSB2* in February 2019. I would have recommended her to see an exhibition I saw in November 2018, which I believe she would have found very helpful. Between 1974 and 1979 a group of photographers, collectively called Exit, took a series of black-and-white photographs in various British cities: Belfast, Glasgow, Middlesbrough, Birmingham and even a few in Holloway! They depict the shocking poverty and brutality caused by Mrs Thatcher's rolling back of the welfare state. One unforgettable shot shows a group of kids – infants, really – in a bleak room with wallpaper peeling off the wall. There is a packet of cereal on the table, but no evidence of milk, sugar or tea. The exhibition was called *Survival*, and although the photography stopped in 1979, things had not changed much when I first visited you in Brafferton Arbor in 1981.

I had never seen poverty like it. I saw living conditions I thought had ended with the 19th century. Bernard Shaw, who at one point worked as a rent collector in Dublin, wrote, 'Poverty is the mother and father of brutality and criminality.' Certainly Sue and Rita possess what Shaw would have characterised as 'Life Force', and their sexual adventure shows a courage and curiosity in the face of these conditions. Far from being a simple saucy schoolgirl romp, their story could be characterised as a bold and determined defiance of insuperable odds. But it is an all-too-brief snapshot of youth. A grim future awaited you both: you were dead of a brain tumour at the age of 29, while Rita (real name Eileen) was dying of emphysema at the age of 53, when the play was being rehearsed last year.

Eileen was interviewed by Stephen Armstrong for his book, *The Road to Wigan Pier Revisited*. She tells him her diet is an apple and three or four cups of tea with sugar a day. 'I've got nothing,' she says. 'I've worked all me life and I've got nothing.' An excerpt from Armstrong's book would have provided a chilling and authentic coda which would have acted as a salutary corrective to a tale of schoolgirl pranks. However, Kate cut it because 'it didn't work'. I certainly understand it would have made an abrasive contrast with a successful populist production featuring prolonged scene changes with choreographed miming to an '80s soundtrack. But the contrast would have been the point.

Pivotal to the play is the figure of Brian, the father, who is portrayed in Alan Clarke's film as a drunken buffoon. In real life he was more like Bill Sykes. I found him seriously scary. You showed me his club made from a broken broomstick handle with insulating tape wound round the splintered end. He used it to whack you kids across the shoulders. Your sister Pamela showed me the bruises on her arms.

In addition to everything else planned for *RSB2* there is usually a commercial production every few years. A recent one was advertised by a cartoon depicting Sue with a bubble coming out of her mouth with a single word, 'Saucy!!!', in it. Certainly your plays, and *RSB2* in particular, have a Chaucerian celebration of sexuality and transgressive behaviour, but Sue, if not Rita, is well aware that Bob is committing a crime for which he could be sent to prison. However, it is the girls' own lusty wit, zest and independence which propels the plot forward ('I could shag the arse off him meself'). The play has survived because it catches with exactitude the manners and moral code of a particular place at a particular time. I hope future productions will respect the entire picture you have so memorably created and not simply settle for the 'Saucy!!!' cartoon.

Since 1981 many schemes to promote new writing have been launched by most theatres – 'access', 'opportunity', 'diversity', 'outreach' are all buzzwords designed to release funds from the Arts Council's treasure chest. But as far as I am aware none has uncovered a talent like yours. It is time to say quite simply that your plays endure because you had a prodigious talent, and they should be produced quite straightforwardly, as you would have wished.

I very much regret that you did not live long enough to write the plays of your maturity. I think they would have been equally extraordinary, and your power of total recall would have been an invaluable guide to any director committed to fulfilling your complete vision.

Yours with respect and admiration,

Max

Marlane Meyer lives in Hollywood, California. She has been writing plays for 35 years. Her produced plays include *Etta Jenks, The Geography of Luck, Kingfish, Moe's Lucky Seven, The Mystery of Attraction* and *The Chemistry of Change.* She has also been a writer/producer for television. These shows include *Nothing Sacred*, the winner of a Peabody Award, *Law & Order: Criminal Intent* and *CSI: Crime Scene Investigation.* She has also been a recipient of the Kesselring Award and the Susan Smith Blackburn Prize.

July 9, 2020

Dear Marlane,

Nostalgia constitutes a significant and often deeply held feeling for many of us in the theatre. I recall two middle-aged actresses reminiscing in a coffee break and evoking the different places they had played. 'Whitby?' said one. 'Ah,' said the other, 'Whitby. I first went blonde in Whitby.'

With all the other playwrights I refer to in this book I have had a prolonged relationship encompassing three, four or five productions spread over a time as long as 30 years. With you I directed just a single play, and you travelled 6,000 miles from Hollywood, California, to inspect a production that had already been prepared, baked and was just being taken out of the oven, so to speak. So you didn't play a large part in rehearsals, but you coped helpfully and graciously with the tricky obligation of encouraging and applauding a group of complete strangers attempting to bring to life a play that you knew intimately. I very much enjoyed the friendship we were pitched into in the course of the one week you were in London, and I regret that we have not kept in touch since then. So the nostalgia I feel about our time together is of a friendship based on the experience of watching your play with you for three consecutive nights, and of one night of serious, convivial drinking.

Etta Jenks begins with a young woman completing a journey. She aspires to be an actress. She believes you have to be yourself as an actress, but, alas, this is not the only necessary requirement. There are many plays that occupy the desolate hinterland located between the ages of 17 and 25. And I have directed several. The protagonists, who have usually left both the shelter of home and also the cloistered academic haven of college or university, find themselves in the big city, where the rules are ill defined and where they have to determine their own priorities, roles and friends. It may often be a time of chaos and confusion in which the availability of drugs and sex is often accompanied by the worrying absence of cash.

Such plays as *Rita, Sue and Bob Too*, Stella Feehily's *Duck*, Robin Soans' *Mixed Up North* and of course Mark Ravenhill's *Shopping and Fucking*, all occupy this dangerous world, which shows characters negotiating the difficult terrain and often getting lost in it. To cope with this world, young people usually coalesce into a new tribal grouping or 'family' which affords some protection. But you parachute Etta into a terrifying 'new family' who are engaged in the pornography industry, or are lurking on the fringes of it.

But far from being a victim in this murky, subterranean world, Etta becomes a player and a manipulator herself. You also added a sprinkling of magic realism which enabled her to escape what Michael Billington of *The Guardian* called 'the hermetic harshness' of this brutal world. Etta Jenks may be a 'badass' bitch, and certainly she's a heroine who is difficult to sympathise with, but in the 1990s a number of women playwrights began to explore flawed female central characters. And you also give Etta the acuity and opportunism that Thackeray, for example, gives to Becky Sharp. The play was fresh and had an original spirit. This was reinforced by Miranda Richardson's bold performance as Etta. Certainly the audience were relieved that Etta didn't end up with concrete galoshes in San Pedro Bay.

Your own experience of the world of pornography was at an unusual and unexpected tangent: your father was in the Merchant Marine, working in Los Angeles Harbor, and you would help him load his launch with pornographic photos and film clips which he would then ferry out to lonely sailors at their deep-water anchorages (53 feet) in San Pedro Bay.

Impressive and articulate, you reminded me of the young women I had encountered at Riverdale Country Day School in the Bronx, where I had spent my 18th year on an English-Speaking Union scholarship. They seemed poised to launch themselves into a glittering and successful orbit through life. Your own particular trajectory veered you away from the theatre and into television, where you became a successful writer and producer, making occasional forays back into the world of theatre.

We had a good evening drinking together, ending up in that fashionable '80s watering hole the Zanzibar, where you gave me a good talking-to. I was complaining about something: the swingeing overtime rates, or perhaps the late arrival of the set, or the parochialism of the critics. 'Why are you always moaning?' you challenged. 'You are doing the job you love, with people you love, and you are being paid to do it. You are in the centre of your life and you should celebrate that.'

You were absolutely right. There is always much to complain about in the theatre, but equally there is much that is fulfilling and joyful. Let's start with the privilege of choosing the work and the people you wish to do it with. And that also includes the opportunity to cross-pollinate and work with people from other cultures. I'm not the kind of conceptual director they go for in Germany, but I have been lucky enough to direct French actors in France, Dutch actors in Holland, Australian actors in Australia, Danish actors in Denmark, Irish actors in Ireland and, on several occasions, American actors in the United States. These occasions have not universally been triumphant, but I have never failed to be challenged by and to learn from them. Perhaps the most important thing I have learned is that the most significant and pertinent work I am likely to undertake is the examination of my own culture and history with a close-knit group of like-minded actors.

It's a long way from San Pedro Bay to Sloane Square, but you made the journey into a treat and a pleasure.

Thank you, Marlane.

As ever,

Max

Sebastian Barry was born in Dublin in 1955. His plays include *Boss Grady's Boys*, *The Steward of Christendom*, *Our Lady of Sligo*, *The Pride of Parnell Street* and *Dallas Sweetman*. His novels include *The Whereabouts of Eneas McNulty*, *Annie Dunne*, *A Long Long Way*, which was shortlisted for the Man Booker Prize, *The Secret Scripture*, also shortlisted for the Man Booker Prize, *On Canaan's Side* and *The Temporary Gentleman*. His awards include the Irish-America Fund Literary Award, the Christopher Ewart-Biggs Prize, and Costa Awards for Best Novel and Book of the Year.

Donal McCann (1943–1999) was an Irish stage, film and television actor. He was widely accepted as the greatest Irish theatre actor of his generation. He gave outstanding performances in Joe Dowling's production of *Faith Healer* and as Joxer in *The Plough and the Stars*. When *The Steward of Christendom* played at the Brooklyn Academy of Music in 1997 *Newsweek* hailed him as a 'world-class actor' and *The New York Times* referred to 'this astonishing Irish actor... widely regarded the finest of them all'.

December 12, 2019

Dear Sebastian,

Last night Stella and I caught up with your public lecture delivered on the stage of the Gate Theatre and later broadcast on RTE. It was an illuminating and heartfelt tribute to Donal McCann, whose searing and unforgettable performance in your play, *The Steward of Christendom*, proved a giddy peak in the theatrical careers of both of us.

I wish I had had a moment to talk with you before the lecture as my recollections, although not substantially different from yours, may have added to the mix. I was shocked when you told the audience that it was 20 years since the performance. Donal is rarely out of my mind. In part that is because one of his gifts to me was a very fine pen-and-ink self-portrait, which hangs in our flat, and I admire it every time I go up the stairs. His other gift on my birthday was an Ireland rugby jersey, which Donal claimed came from his accountant, Brendan Sherry, who, like Donal, was an ex-Terenure player and was also a one-cap wonder for Ireland. Donal later told me that his account of the origin of the jersey was a fiction, but I prefer the fiction myself!

I first worked with Donal when I directed Tom Kilroy's *Tea and Sex and Shakespeare* at the Abbey. It was a relatively smooth experience and we got on well. It is only with the wisdom of hindsight that I realise it was the sole production I worked on with Donal where he was completely sober from beginning to end. He was a recovering alcoholic, but on the other two productions he was a not-so-recovering alcoholic.

The second production we did together was *A Prayer for My Daughter* by Thomas Babe in the Theatre Upstairs. The week before rehearsals were scheduled to start, Donal's London agent rang to say that Donal had gone missing but that he was 'probably' in London. Over the weekend I waited for further news. None came. On the Monday morning we gathered in the Theatre Upstairs. The other members of the cast were Tony Sher, John Dicks and Kevin McNally. Ten o'clock… no Donal. By 10.30 we had exhausted small talk and I was reluctantly approaching the decision that if we were to proceed any further I would have to read the part myself when Donal burst through the door. He was haggard, unshaven and in a severe state of disrepair. I learned later from Gary Lilburn, an ex-colleague of Donal's, that at this period of his life the mode Donal adopted was to go on 'a monumental batter' immediately prior to rehearsal, before adopting a rigorous abstinence for the whole period of rehearsal and the run, ending with a further 'monumental batter' after the concluding performance. It was a discipline that Donal adhered to strictly.

Sans apology and with only a cursory nod towards introductions, Donal launched into a bravura performance with the sweat dripping down his face. He was playing an alcoholic Irish American New York cop and his aggression filled and overflowed in the Theatre Upstairs. He was unknown to the English actors, but they were also unknown to him. John Dicks and Kevin McNally are exceptionally fine and talented actors, while Tony Sher was well on the way to becoming a theatre star. Donal had thrown down the gauntlet and they responded with readings of equal energy and charisma.

I don't remember a great deal about the rest of the rehearsal period, but I think as director all I had to do was tactfully manage the energy and harness it. There was an unexpected and moving moment when Donal's aggressive cop revealed his unhappiness at the hostility and alienation of his teenage daughter. He embraced the near-naked drug addict, played by Kevin McNally, as a substitute. At this distance in time I don't remember why Kevin was naked but naked he certainly was. In the Dublin Festival this was the moment when Hugh Leonard, the distinguished Irish playwright and Director of the Dublin Festival, happened to make a pastoral visit. He had intended to stay for only a few minutes before making other visits. However, he realised immediately that his departure at this point would be widely interpreted as a gesture of disgust and moral disapproval. By the end of the scene he was so gripped by the characters and by the narrative that he stayed loyally to the end.

The third production together was *The Steward of Christendom*. Of course Donal could be difficult, even alarming, but he knew he wanted a director and he wanted the director to be of the highest quality. He would conduct a rigorous check before admitting you to the team. He was not a vain man, but he had a just assessment of his own extraordinary talent and he wanted to ensure that the director – and everybody else, for that matter – was up to scratch. He asked me discreetly but with some urgency and concern if I thought you were as good a playwright as Brian Friel. Later that same evening you told me he had asked you if you thought I was as good a director as Michael Attenborough. This was setting the bar pretty high, as Mike had just triumphed with *Observe the Sons of Ulster Marching Towards the Somme*. The bottom line was pretty clear: were we good enough to help him?

There were rules, too. Normally I stopped for lunch at around one o'clock, but on one particular day I was on a bit of a roll and continued to 1.30. After lunch Donal said tersely, 'I want a word with you.' It sounded ominous, but rehearsals had been going pretty well. At the end of the afternoon I said, 'Yes, what is it, Donal?' He said, 'Don't you ever do that to me again.' I had no idea how I had transgressed. He continued, 'I went into that bar. I ordered two vodkas and put them on the piano. I didn't touch them for ten minutes. "That'll teach Max," I said. He thought I had been taunting him by prolonging the morning session and preventing his customary fuel stop. You may have noticed that I stopped for lunch pretty sharply after that.

Donal wanted rehearsals to be organised and purposeful. They were scheduled to start in London after Christmas, but Donal had requested an extra week by himself to familiarise himself with the text and the shape of the play. It was a mammoth part and a reasonable enough request.

Trinity College Dublin, an alma mater for both you and I, made a large room available in the Museum Building, overlooking the rugby pitch. What they didn't reveal was that they turned off the central heating during the vacation. It was freezing and miserable, and the three of us huddled together in the arctic conditions. I wanted to be at home organising Christmas and I guess I must have been whingeing a bit. One chilly morning I met Donal in the middle of Front Square on the way to rehearsal. 'Just get on with it,' he said. 'This country gave you your education. It's time you gave something back.' He was joking, but only partly.

Rehearsals for him had an almost sacrosanct quality, and once you had been admitted to the team he was really committed. He had a surprising graciousness that embraced us all. I recall giving him a rather woolly note about a particular scene. He put his hand on my shoulder. 'My dear Max,' he said, 'I would do it exactly as you wish except that I haven't a fucking clue what you're talking about.' The lesson for me here was: 'Be more direct if you dare.' He was very disciplined in performance and monastic in his preparation, but he also had a mischievous unpredictability that kept us all on edge. He alarmed Out of Joint's young producer, Sonia Friedman, by taking a taxi from Euston to the Theatre Royal, Brighton. He claimed he was a stranger to London and couldn't be expected to navigate from Euston to Victoria. In Liverpool he appeared for the curtain call with a long Everton scarf around his neck, thrilling half the audience but alienating the Liverpool supporters.

The last note I ever gave him was unwisely at the first-night party following the opening night at the Brooklyn Academy of Music. *The Steward of Christendom* had put on two or three minutes, and I thought Donal was slowing down his delivery to accommodate an American audience. Donal told me to fuck off. The next day I flew back to London. A few days afterwards, late one evening, I was phoned by the stage manager. The performance was about to start in Brooklyn. 'Donal wants a word,' she said. I prepared myself for a verbal assault – but no, he was all charm again. 'You were quite right,' he said. 'But I've had a word with Rory and everything is fine now.' Rory Murray played a young RIC (Royal Irish Constabulary) recruit who appeared in one scene that lasted three minutes, while Donal never left the stage!

The Steward of Christendom was a big success and it is totally appropriate, 20 years later, to celebrate Donal's achievement. The play transferred to Downstairs at the Royal Court and went to New York and to the Sydney and New Zealand Festivals. And yet it was a production I approached with considerable trepidation, unsure I knew how to direct it. It was a play I had always wanted to programme at the Royal Court, but I was not convinced I was the right director. Sometimes it seemed to me that your great lyrical gifts had overwhelmed your dramatic instincts. But having worked twice with Donal before, I had some idea of his prodigious talent and range, and I thought if I could get him on board I might just undertake the voyage.

Donal was on location in Yorkshire and we had nightly conversations in which he declined to make a clear commitment. One evening he said, 'I don't think I would wear slippers. I would be taking them on and off all evening as I get in and out of bed. I'll wear socks.' He was already visualising his performance. I took this to be a hugely positive sign. Donal collected gestures too: when his character, Thomas Dunne, was tired he would stand with his legs slightly apart and with his hands resting on top of his head. He told me he had captured the gesture from a Terenure rugby player who went on playing after he should have retired and stood in the line-out taking his ease as best he could before rejoining the game.

My other contribution before rehearsals started was a deft piece of editing. I prompted you to conclude the play with the story of the young Thomas securing a reprieve for a dog who had been condemned for worrying sheep. Thomas and the dog stay in the freezing wood all night before coming down to the farm in the early morning for a reconciliation with his worried father. This provided an emotional wallop at the end, which Joe Papp would have termed 'an 11 o'clock ending'. But I was still my own third-choice director after others had turned it down. The lesson here is that sometimes you have to start the race without being able to see the finishing post. Because once we started work the play miraculously revealed itself and I found I did know how to direct it after all.

Sometimes at post-show discussions, or at workshops with students, I am asked, 'What is your favourite production?' It's a mischievous and tricky question, because success carries its own allure. So *Top Girls*, *Our Country's Good*, *Serious Money*, *Feelgood*, *The Permanent Way* and, of course, *The Steward of Christendom* feature prominently in every answer. But *Rat in the Skull*, *Crouch, Touch, Pause, Engage*, *This May Hurt a Bit*, *Talking to Terrorists* and *A Dish of Tea with Dr Johnson* have given me equal pleasure.

'Who is your favourite actor? or 'Who is the best actor you have ever worked with?' are even more hazardous and divisive questions. There is, of course, a bejewelled necklace of famous actors, some of whom a young audience may recognise. These would include Wally Shawn, Alec Baldwin, Tony Sher, Linda Hunt, Lesley Manville, Andrew Garfield, Gary Oldman, Brian Cox, Tom Wilkinson, Alan Rickman, Anna Massey, Lynn Redgrave, Julianne Moore, Harriet Walter, Nicola Walker and Suranne Jones. But on other occasions I might list that precious semi-permanent company of faithful and favourite actors, perhaps not yet so celebrated, but equally talented, that every director carries in his head and in his heart. Among these would be Ian Redford, Tony Rohr, Pearce Quigley, David Beames, Lloyd Hutchinson, David Westhead, Patrick Brennan, Sally Rogers, Linda Bassett, Bethan Witcomb, Deborah Findlay, Frances Barber, Kate Ashfield, Jane Wymark, David Rintoul, June Watson, Danny Webb, Monica Dolan, Ron Cook, Paul Jesson, Paul Freeman, Catherine Russell, Mossie Smith, Franc Ashman, Katherine O'Reilly, Danny Sapani and Jason Watkins. But on other occasions I find myself saying, 'Donal McCann.' Quite simply, 'Donal McCann.'

Best wishes,

Love,

Max

Caryl Churchill is widely regarded as one of the most significant and influential playwrights working today. The author of more than 30 plays, she has reshaped the theatre landscape and continues to produce adventurous new work.

January 18, 2020

Dearest Caryl,

I'm a bit wary about writing to you as I know how keen you are that your work should speak for itself rather than be subjected to interpretation or interpolation. You once said people went to watch football matches without having to have the game explained to them, and why couldn't plays be treated in the same manner? I agreed, but of course we have both been proved completely wrong: in the event, football and rugby matches are preceded by hours of punditry and followed by many wise words about how a particular team should have played.

In your final year at Oxford in 1960 you contributed an article on theatre to a magazine called *XXth Century*. It amounted to a powerful manifesto in which you criticised the kitchen-sink theatre of the '50s for its conservatism of form, and its content for lack of ambition. You called it the 'age of the small statement'. You wrote that theatre should be making major statements and you called for daring experimentation in form. The manifesto is bold enough for someone commencing a career at the age of 21, but what is even more remarkable is how you have sustained this position in an extraordinarily fertile and prolific career over nearly 60 years. No playwright has ever been more daring and more innovative, or has tackled so many daunting subjects, from climate change and despoliation of the planet to the privatisation of the money markets.

I once asked Edward Bond if he had been influenced by Beckett. He dismissed the question disdainfully. But the following day, in a more conciliatory mood, he said quietly, 'No, not Beckett, but all of us were influenced by Ionesco, I think.' Perhaps you too were taken with the possibilities of absurdism. Your work has always embraced both the comic and the political possibilities of the surreal. I remember on one occasion, probably after an arduous afternoon at the coalface struggling with actions, you telling me gently, 'They aren't called plays for nothing. It is possible to be playful.' And you always have been.

We first met in or around the Royal Court in 1972 when *Owners*, directed by Nicky Wright, was in the Theatre Upstairs. I had finished work with the Traverse Workshop Company and, while directing *The Beggar's Opera* at the Nottingham Playhouse, had stayed at a large house outside Nottingham, to which a small chapel was adjoined. In it was the tomb of a 15th-century Crusader who had made the journey to the Holy Land. On his return he married and had five children and lived the life of a prosperous farmer. I was intrigued by the gaps in his story. Did he tell his son about his visit to the Church of the

Holy Sepulchre? Did he walk down the Via Dolorosa? Did he sit one sunny afternoon in the Garden of Gethsemane, looking at the ancient olive trees?

I approached you in early 1976 with the idea of a workshop in which we might take the story further. You were sufficiently intrigued to agree, although I don't think I was clear about what a workshop could achieve. I recruited a lively group of actors, partly formed of my old colleagues from Edinburgh, and we started work. I realised very quickly that you were not simply super-bright, but you possessed a rare theatrical intelligence and perception. I had gathered from somewhere – Nicky Wright, perhaps – that you had attained a double first at Oxford, and I was suitably impressed and intimidated. Later I think I passed this information on to *The New York Times* in an interview, so it may well be appended to your CV by now. Some 30 years later you told me that I had perpetrated a fiction. No matter. I prefer my version, and to me you will always have a well-deserved double first.

After ten days or so you proposed a radical change of direction. You had been exploring literature about religion, and particularly ecstatic religion. You had read Christopher Hill's *The World Turned Upside Down* and thought it provided an even more encompassing story. Intimidated by your double first, I surrendered wisely and immediately. Inspired by stories such as that of Jenny Geddes, who defied the structure of the church in 1637 when she threw a stool at the Dean of St Giles Cathedral in Edinburgh, shouting, '*Deil colic the wame o' ye, fause thief; daur ye say Mass in my lug?*'

We explored eccentricities and radical beliefs. The actors were placed in a social situation: in church, with a midwife, or at the flour mill, for example. They were given two playing cards. Whoever got the joker as one of their cards had to be eccentric to the power of the other card they held. A nine or ten meant they were 'ecstatic' and obliged to 'talk in tongues'. Millennial groups in England from the mid-17th century included the Quakers and the Levellers, but there were many groups who believed in the radical transformation of society. During the two-week workshop, most of us in the group began to understand what you had seen from the beginning: that this was yet another English revolution that didn't quite happen.

The script that evolved from the workshop was entirely your work but drew on the inventiveness of the actors and on the playfulness we had all experienced together. In *The Joint Stock Book* you wrote: 'Each actor had to draw from a lucky dip of Bible texts and get up at once and preach, urging some extraordinary course of action justified from the Bible.' 'Suffer the little children to come unto me' became an impassioned plea to lay the children in the street and run them over with a steamroller. The actors drew cards and had to be eccentric to the power of that number and were then put in a public place – a department store, a doctor's waiting room, a hairdresser's – until it was clear who it was and how they were breaking convention. You wrote, 'I'd never seen an exercise or improvisation before and I was as thrilled as a child at a pantomime. I had an intense pleasure in it all.'

With hindsight I am now able to see more clearly what

I was unaware of at the time – that you were also writing about the failure of idealism in poor Jim Callaghan's Labour government. Currently the air is full of the sound of pattering feet as the Labour Party scurries towards the centre ground, discarding principles and policies as they go. Then, as now, the English have an innate conservatism that is resistant to a radical transformation of society. Perhaps *Light Shining in Buckinghamshire* is even more pertinent in 2020 than it was in 1976.

The next play we did together was *Cloud Nine*, in 1979. This started with a workshop too. You suggested we start with the subject of sexual politics. I have written about the workshop extensively in *Taking Stock* (2007). Reading both the book and my notes taken at the time once more, I am stunned by the integrity and candour with which the actors revealed and discussed extraordinarily vulnerable moments from their own lives. It was challenging work. As one actor observed sagely at the end of the workshop, 'It's not a subject you can tame.' History has proved her right. We began with the difficult task of exposing ourselves and our own sexuality, but I think a remark made by Dave Hill early in the course of the workshop may have been influential. He said, 'We should not just talk about our own lives. We come from a generation whose parents were repressed sexually and we are bound to start with that.'

This may have been one of a number of moments that prompted you so imaginatively to set the first act in Victorian Africa. In retrospect, I think the workshop was more useful in raising the collective consciousness of the group than it was in elucidating the topic to you.

Unlike the workshops for both *LS in B* and *Serious Money* – which explored subjects of which we were all ignorant – *Cloud Nine* started with issues that involved us all and which began with our own families. We placed women in typical male environments of the day (a boardroom) and the men in a beauty salon. One actress impersonated a gay Labour MP facing a reselection committee in her local constituency. 'I have nothing against this MP,' said Julie Covington as the chairperson, 'but we have to decide whether or not she will help the party in the coming election.' The 'MP' was not reselected.

Cloud Nine also gave me my first glimpse of the possibilities of verbatim theatre. You and I interviewed an actor who gave us an unforgettable account of the expertise required to select a candidate at Waterloo Station for anonymous and immediate oral sex in the seclusion of a slam-door carriage on the 13-minute journey to Clapham Junction.

In the workshop itself we also interviewed the caretaker of the Tower Theatre Canonbury, where we were rehearsing. She was a forbidding figure, laying down the law about washing cups and closing the rehearsal room on the dot of 6pm, but the power of her story affected us all: 'Within an hour of getting married, Nick hit me across the face. He put me in hospital seven times. In those days you had to put up with it, dear.' Finally he kicked her into the fridge, knocking her unconscious, when her split shopping bag had smeared butter on the seat of his car. After she came round she told him to clear out. They didn't speak for a day and on the Monday he emptied the fridge, taking his car. 'I haven't seen or spoken to him from that day to this.' Eventually she was wooed by a lorry driver at the canning factory where she was working in the canteen. They courted for a year but didn't have sex in that time because he had been nursing a sick wife for ten years and couldn't get an erection. 'Finally we did it one night and both of us had an organism [sic]. That's terrific. It was the first one I ever had in my life and I was 59. Now we have it sometimes as much as twice in one week and I'm on cloud nine.'

The brutality at the heart of her story shocked and moved us. The whole two-week period was sometimes more akin to a therapy session than to a theatrical experience. It had been unexpectedly traumatic, but it bonded a disparate group of talented actors who obviously felt some ownership of the material.

Joint Stock had been fumbling towards becoming a collective following our politicisation in the course of rehearsing *Fanshen*. In the subsequent *Epsom Downs*, by Howard Brenton, we endeavoured to cast the play by mutual and collective decisions. Unsurprisingly it led to a great deal of friction and disagreement, although it has to be said that the final result was unexpectedly successful. Wilfully or foolishly, we elected to follow the same route with *Cloud Nine*.

The casting pressure from the actors must have been enormous for you. The fragile unity of the group was strained as a couple of actors vied for the same part. Bill Hoyland wanted his role expanded, and Tony Sher, with an infallible nose for farcical possibilities, pressured for the high comedy of the first half to be sustained throughout the whole play. But you held on to the reins, commenting at one point, 'I can see a perfectly horrible play emerging.' Your calm but authoritative words instantly quelled the fires of revolution.

One of your most practical theatrical gifts is that you are an excellent and astute editor, and after a week of performances you cut some ten minutes from the second half and a further five minutes from the first half of *Cloud Nine*. You were to respond even more quickly to an early run-though of *Serious Money* in the rehearsal room by cutting much of the music and reshaping the first half entirely. Both decisions improved and streamlined the respective plays.

Your immediate response as soon as the plays were in front of you was enormously impressive. Nor did the success of *Cloud Nine* at the Royal Court bring its customary balm. Ian Albery, a commercial theatre producer, was keen to transfer the play but demanded further cuts, which we all resisted. Bill Hoyland and Carole Hayman were particularly keen to transfer, but Julie Covington was clear that a West End run would damage the work and was determined to avoid the fame and stardom which was so clearly beckoning her at this point.

Top Girls followed four years later, prompted by Mrs Thatcher's accession to power in 1979. We have talked about this, and our recollections are slightly different. Perhaps that's hardly surprising since it was 37 years ago. But my memory is that after you delivered the initial draft of the script we went for a walk together down

Royal Hospital Road and into the Physic Garden. I was despondent, because although I liked the script very much I knew that there was no way the Royal Court had the resources any longer to produce a play with 17 actors. It was a sunny afternoon and we sat on the grass in front of a eucalyptus tree while you patiently explained that you had designed the play to be doubled, and that it could be performed by seven actors. I think the stunning dinner party that formed the first scene was still in the form of separate monologues, and your plans to intercut them and turn them into conversation had only just started. I was much relieved, and there was a new spring in my step on the walk back to Sloane Square.

The play is an eccentric jigsaw puzzle, with what is chronologically the first scene coming last. There are a number of separate worlds: the dinner party of the first scene in which Marlene's promotion to managing director is celebrated by a formidable and surreal assembly of women from myth and history. Secondly there is the slightly spooky and imaginative world of the den in the back garden in Suffolk occupied by Kit (aged 12) and Angie (16). And then there is the piratical, competitive world of the office, before the play returns to East Anglia and concludes in a confrontation between Marlene and Joyce. It is only on page 76 out of 95 that the audience will learn that Marlene, and not Joyce, is Angie's birth mother.

The play functions like a Rembrandt triptych. Each panel is a complete and detailed picture, but the combination of the whole forms an emotionally overwhelming and politically penetrating whole. I am always optimistic once I have committed to directing a play, and I always thought *Top Girls* was a particularly fine play, but did I know at the time that it was one of the great plays of the 20th century and would endure as part of the national repertoire? I think that was unknowable.

However, in the '90s I had a subscription to the Classic Car Club which allowed me to borrow Ferraris, Aston Martins and Lamborghinis from their fleet. On one occasion I had a very beautiful late '40s Rolls-Royce for a weekend. It would be simplistic and misleading to state that the car drove itself, but it certainly took responsibility for major decisions, and its incredible Getrag gearbox changed gear with a flawless sense of timing, while the steering was firm but feather-light. Directing a major classic can be like driving a Rolls-Royce. I had this experience when directing *King Lear* and *The Recruiting Officer* at the Royal Court, but I was first to have this sensation with *Top Girls*. Of course you can go wrong with a classic, and it's just about possible to stall a Rolls-Royce. But if you're able to get a couple of scenes right then the play takes over and guides you to the next decision.

The play's reputation accrued slowly. The first notices were good and houses at the Royal Court were certainly respectable. The play moved to New York in December 1982, where Joe Papp enthusiastically and shamelessly billed it as a London hit and we played to packed houses. There is no better or happier place in the world if you have a hit than New York. It opens its doors and its heart to you. So Christmas 1982 in that great city was one of the happiest times ever. We were able to return to the Royal

Court in 1983 for a run which I was able to bill legitimately as a New York hit, while the play continued at the Public Theater with an American cast.

By the mid-'80s I thought that the Royal Court had covered the ground with plays about people who had no money, and it was time to examine another sector of the community. I approached you with an idea about researching a play set in or around the financial markets. It was a stroke of luck that the financial sector was at this time going through the convulsions of deregulation. After another workshop you wrote *Serious Money* – the fourth of your great plays on such different subjects and in such different theatrical styles. To direct four plays of yours would have been a peak in anybody's career, and it certainly was in mine. *Serious Money* was particularly attached to its time in the late '80s, but the other three plays have been revived regularly.

Academics and critics have quite rightly commented widely on your extraordinary inventiveness and your ability to play with form like a conjuror drawing a string of coloured handkerchiefs out of a hat that have miraculously turned into a rabbit. But this playfulness is combined with a clarity of purpose and a compelling moral conviction. Recently Danny Boyle wrote to me, 'We all dream, so often foolishly, that our work will change the world.' Certainly your Oxford manifesto sets forth with that bold expectation.

I think after *Serious Money* you were already disappointed that the theatre was so manifestly ineffective at changing things, and some time later you wrote a series of plays which you termed anti-plays which self-destructed in spectacular fashion. *Blue Heart* repeated itself with alternative conclusions, while the language itself was infected by a virus and ended in a series of spluttering consonants: 'Bbb kk b.' But not for one moment did you lose your sense of humour. In fact *Blue Heart* is one of the funniest plays I have ever been involved with. Pearce Quigley's entrance as a reverse-jointed ostrich walking backwards was super-hilarious.

However, after our date in Brooklyn our next engagement was at the university town of Coimbra in Portugal. The actors arrived safely but the costumes were delayed somewhere over the Atlantic and we were forced to hire a gorilla costume from a local fancy-dress emporium. The gorilla smelt strongly of BO and the fur had come off in patches. It was 'super-hilarious' only to other members of the company, who enjoyed Pearce's discomfiture. But it must have been puzzling for the poor Portuguese audience.

One of the alternative conclusions to *Blue Heart* involved a crowd of kids (six, seven or eight years of age) bursting out of a cupboard and rushing offstage. We recruited the children in each country we played in. Children from the Catholic countries such as Portugal, Italy and Ireland were the most biddable and disciplined. But in Finland primary-school education started very late, about seven or so, at which point they learned three languages in five years. But at six the children were quite wild, and it was like trying to direct a mob of feral elves. In Israel I felt as if I was directing part of the Old Testament:

'Elijah and Abraham, please leave the cupboard door open until Malachi and Jacob come out. No, Ishmael, don't pull Rebecca's hair, please.'

At the same time you distrusted the 11 o'clock ending, when the world's problems all appear to be solved if the convicts get the play on, or if the lad gets to the Royal Ballet school, and you became an expert at the equivocal and disturbing ending. Who can forget the last words of *Top Girls* as Angie descends the stairs saying, 'Frightening, frightening,' and sees a future in which things will become less and less equal for those who are not Top Girls? Or Ian Dury's cynical and bitter anthem which concluded *Serious Money: Five More Glorious Years,* an ironic celebration of the Tory victory, even more pertinent in 2019 than it was in 1987. But my particular pick would be the melancholic conclusion of *Light Shining in Buckinghamshire,* when Briggs – all revolutionary idealism dissipated, all passion gone – tells the audience directly that he now has no expectations that Christ will come again, but that he has trained himself to eat and digest grass and leads a quiet, solitary life in the corner of a friendly farmer's meadow. That fine actor, Nigel Terry, was ever the master of the melancholic, elegiac moment, and as the lights faded on his solitude the moment never ceased to be unbearably moving.

So perhaps the world hasn't changed as significantly as you would have wished, but what has transformed completely is the theatre itself. David Edgar, a consistent, probing voice, provided a cogent analysis at a theatre conference in Valencia: 'At the beginning of the '80s there were two prominent female playwrights, Pam Gems and Caryl Churchill. But by the end of the decade they had been joined by more than half a dozen others.' These would include Claire McIntyre, Sarah Daniels, Shelagh Stephenson, Sharman McDonald, Charlotte Keatley and Andrea Dunbar.

Thirty years later they have been joined by several dozen more. In addition, every major new writing theatre in London – with the exception of the National Theatre – now has a woman as Artistic Director, and at the National itself both the Head of New Writing and the Literary Manager are posts filled by women. In addition, several of the most significant new writing theatres in the regions – Bolton, Liverpool and Edinburgh – have female Artistic Directors. You have undoubtedly been the leader and the inspiration for a revolution that has utterly changed the theatrical landscape. At the entrance to St Paul's Cathedral is Christopher Wren's monument. It reads:

'*Si monumentum requiris, circumspice.*' If you want a monument, look about you. It could be equally fitting for you if placed on a plaque behind the Royal Court box office.

As ever,

Love,

Max

MY FAMILY

My second wife, Ann Pennington, and I adopted **Kitty Stafford-Clark** from Bulgaria in 1989. Kitty is an accomplished stage manager and producer.

May 3, 2019

Dearest Kitty,

It's a bit strange to be writing to you, since you left here only an hour ago. You were in a cheerful, perky mood, in part, I think, because Arsenal beat Valencia 3-1 last night, but also, I think, because you have given in your notice at your current job and resolved to change your future. You have always been very strong-minded and determined and I admire that.

I first met you when you were six months old, in an orphanage in Sofia, Bulgaria. A large and airy ward was filled with about 30 cots, and two apron-clad babushkas were doing a round of nappy-changing. When they got to one end they started again at the other, like painting the Forth Bridge.

The orphanage was in the centre of a pretty bleak housing estate, but very far from those horrible and squalid workhouses depicted at that time in documentaries about Romania. Ann and I were interviewed by the matron at her glass-topped desk in a neat but small office. She explained in excellent English and perfect French that the orphanage was a state facility provided for this particular housing estate. If young people got into trouble they were able to board children in the orphanage and reclaim them if their circumstances changed at a later date. In your case, your birth parents had made a more permanent deposit, as it were. Your mother was 16 and your father an engineering student, the matron told us. She gave us her blessing and we gave the orphanage a washing machine. So that's what you cost: a washing machine. What value!

Your adoption was approved by the Bulgarian courts and British Airways didn't raise an eyebrow at our returning to London with an extra passenger. You slept for the whole flight. Things were not so smooth at Heathrow. The customs officer was edgy and uncertain. Apparently there had been no previous adoptions from Bulgaria and he was clearly reluctant to set a precedent. 'You do realise,' he said tersely, 'that I could send this child back to Sofia on the next plane?' Meanwhile, in the next booth an even more ominous interview was proceeding. I could clearly hear the nasal tones and estuary accent of the customs officer: 'So, Mr Nazeem, do you wish me to investigate this so-called cousin of yours in Uxbridge, or is this just another of your little fictions?' I couldn't hear the mumbled reply, but clearly things weren't looking so good for Mr Nazeem. Our officer, however, crumbled in the face of our overwhelmingly obvious middle-classness and granted you a three-month temporary visa.

During this period we had to appear before a district judge in chambers and plead your case. Driving back to

Camden Town I began to relax a bit, but Ann was still, I think, fairly tense. It had, after all, been a pretty nerve-racking few days. There was only one person in the car who seemed completely at ease and that was the six-month-old you! I could see you in the rear-view mirror, ensconced in the throne of the new child seat, recently purchased at Brent Cross. You were grinning and smiling with pleasure at the changing patterns of light and shade as we turned off the motorway and passed under some trees.

We had also been instructed to contact Camden Social Services, and the young woman assigned to your case seemed suspicious and distant. Her main concern appeared to be the steps we would be taking to preserve your Bulgarian cultural heritage. The judge, however, was very impressive. When the four of us (Max, Ann, Kitty and the social worker) kept our appointment in his chambers off Marylebone High Street the first thing he did was remove his wig and put it in one of those dinky tin boxes that lawyers have. The extraordinary act of a gentleman apparently taking off his hair made you coo with delight. He sat at a big partner's desk with a large bookcase behind him. He explained again in some detail that this was a finely balanced case and that his ruling would be creating a precedent.

Apparently, under Bulgarian law a mother is able to give up a child for adoption immediately after giving birth, and this is what your mother had done. Under English law, however, a gap of five weeks after the birth is required before a mother's decision is recognised as legally binding. His honour took down two hefty volumes from the bookcase behind him and quoted two different judgements made in adoption cases over the previous 30 years. One judge had ruled against an adoption from, I think, Nigeria, and one had ruled favourably on a proposed adoption from Georgia. At this point you lost interest in the proceedings, slipped off Ann's knee and, with considerable athleticism, crawled across the floor and under the judge's desk. He was completely unfazed by the unexpected turn of events and scooped you off the carpet and into his arms. 'So, young woman, you would like a word, would you?' he said. Turning to us he said, 'Well, of course I am going to rule in your favour, but I wanted you to know that the law is a very fine instrument and takes these matters very seriously. Parenthood is a great and awesome responsibility. Very good luck to you all.' And so saying he crossed the room with you in his arms and returned you to Ann's lap.

As you know, I haven't been a perfect father, and when you were 15, Ann and I separated and subsequently got divorced. I know how upset you were at the time. Still, we have remained close and I think you know how much I love you.

I was worried about becoming a father. Perhaps because David, my own father, had made so excellent a job of adoption and I was scared of the comparison. I knew it would be a serious responsibility, of course, but I had little idea of what constant pleasure and delight you would afford. You have been particularly constant and supportive over this last year since I was asked to step down from Out of Joint. A real pal.

In recent weeks you've taken on the arduous task of personal trainer, and you monitor my progress on the exercise bike in the gym. Two days ago I astonished us both by doing four miles in ten minutes – a new world record! 'Keep breathing, Dad, keep breathing!' you urged, as I gasped my way beyond eight minutes. It was excellent advice, and I resolve to keep breathing for some time to come.

There is a coda. We had done our best to preserve your Bulgarian heritage, and I had urged you to support Bulgaria in the World Cup in 1995 when you were six. With your help I think they reached the quarter finals. Some years later I picked you up in the car from primary school one afternoon. 'Daddy,' you said seriously, 'do you mind if I don't support Bulgaria anymore? I would like to support Arsenal now.' And you have been a committed Gooner ever since.

As always, all my love,
Kool Dad

Stella Feehily is an Irish actress and author. We got married on August 12, 2010.

July 15, 2018

Dearest Stella,

Together we have outfaced Triumph and Disaster, as well as their best friends Fame and Notoriety.

On Boxing Day 2017, I fell, fracturing my hip and breaking my pelvis. Every morning for the next two wintry months I surfaced in the Cavell Ward of the Whittington Hospital, surrounded by other elderly patients. One old geezer used to design leather trousers for Bon Jovi, another was a television comedy star of the '70s and '80s, and another man didn't know who the fuck he was and kept throwing chairs at nurses. To add to the fun we all got hospital-acquired pneumonia. It was a grim time, alleviated only by the certain knowledge that you were tripping up Whittington Hill with freshly squeezed orange juice and solace. You had already led me steadfastly away from my own near encounter with the Grim Reaper in 2006.

I used to tell you a story about how when I was little I trusted my father so much that I would jump off fences and walls and expect him to be there to catch me. Then one day I thought it would be fun to jump off a seven-foot-high sea wall and call out as I was hurtling down. He caught me as he always did, but in retrospect he was greatly alarmed. You have caught me too, and I'm sorry I didn't tell you I was jumping. Forgive me. In you I have truly found the love I don't deserve.

From the beginning everybody except me perceived there was a considerable age gap between us. In the early days of our courtship we went for Sunday lunch in Howth. Walking around the pleasant harbour afterwards, a group of young men came towards us. As they passed, one leaned towards me and said, 'Jaysus, mister, you muss be loaded.' Since then many people, from taxi drivers to hospital porters, have complimented you on the kindly way you look after your father. I have grown accustomed to it and it now vexes you more than it does me.

After I had a stroke in 2006 the difference became more accentuated, and for the past 12 years you have been saddled with the thankless job of carer. During this time I have never once dressed myself (socks are all I can manage) or done up my own shoelaces. Such is the extent of my independence. Being full-time carer to an elderly raspberry** was not on the agenda when we started living together and it is an immense tribute to you that you took on the job without hesitation. Perhaps it's a tribute to us both that people often do not perceive the extent of my dependence. Even the most sensitive of stage managers would enquire if you were coming with me as Out of Joint prepared to open in Bolton,

---

** 'Raspberry' is a term I gathered from the musician Ian Dury. It derives from cockney rhyming slang: raspberry ripple = cripple. Ian called the disabled toilets 'the raspberries'.

Bristol or Bury St Edmunds, as if it were possible for me to travel or function without you.

When we were in New York for the reading of your play *Dreams of Violence*, that lovely actor Sam Robards asked me a rather peculiar question: 'Is there an upside?' I thought for a minute and said, 'Well, I do get priority boarding on planes, and I don't have to go fucking jogging anymore.' It was a flippant answer, but it contained a truth. I'd been ridiculously reluctant to discard the last vestiges of athleticism, and would go jogging at least twice a week around Regent's Park or Hampstead Heath. You pointed out to me that I often looked terrible and purple on my return and asked me on several occasions to have a medical check-up. (Foolishly, I didn't.) But year by year my times had got slower and it was a relief to stop.

But since then we have had great times travelling. Do you remember the train whistle at night at the beautiful wee hotel in Vermont? The ridiculous ice bath in the production of *Duck* in Hamburg? Or the walk through Minneapolis to find a diner for Sunday brunch? Or the Raffles Hotel and the tiger fruit? Or lunch at Icebergs overlooking Bondi Beach, watching the surfers ride in? Huevos rancheros in Mexico City? Or the craggy faces of my former classmates at the reunion of the class of 1960 at Riverdale Country Day School in the Bronx? Or the equally craggy faces of my former teammates at the 150th anniversary of the founding of Edinburgh Wanderers and the celebratory dinner at Murrayfield? And, of course, the unforgettable occasion when we first met, in a bar called Bond at the bottom of Lower Abbey St in Dublin.

After three drinks I had to return to the Abbey Theatre for a preview of Sebastian Barry's *Hinterland*. As I left the warmth of the bar and stepped into a rainy Lower Abbey St I said, 'I feel as if I've been kicked out of paradise.' That night I read eight scenes of your play, *Duck*, which I subsequently commissioned.

I should tell you once more that *Duck* is one of only four unsolicited plays programmed by Out of Joint in 23 years. During this time I read about 1,400 new plays. For an artistic director there are two great sins: the sin of commission, i.e. those plays I have done which I ought not to have done, and the sin of omission, i.e. those plays I have passed on which I ought to have championed. About the first both tact and shame demand I remain silent, but on the second I am able to be more candid, and there are several plays I passed on which were subsequently hailed. When Dr Johnson was asked by a lady why he had defined 'pastern' incorrectly as the knee of a horse, he replied, 'Ignorance, dear madam. Pure ignorance.' I advance the same defence: I declined an invitation to direct Caryl Churchill's *The Skriker* because I simply did not know how to do it – 'Ignorance, dear Caryl. Pure ignorance.' All I would add is that I have subsequently seen three productions of *The Skriker*, and those three directors didn't know how to direct it either!

However, I did on the first reading think I knew how to direct your first play, *Duck*. It was funny, original and it had a mischievous vein of surreal humour. My confidence, however, was a little misplaced. After a fruitful week of 'actioning' the play around the table I got into trouble with the staging of the first scene. Two totally drunk young women get involved in setting fire to the jeep belonging to the boyfriend of one of them. He happens to be a dangerous drug dealer. The scene demands a teetering balance of reality, wit, danger and farce, and after a couple of uninspired attempts I was glad to hand it over to you. You staged it with confidence and panache. I fully understood that I was working with a young woman whose vision was precise and all-encompassing. I failed to declare your influence when Mark Ravenhill told us it was his favourite scene.

Since then I have directed a further four plays of yours and it has become an increasingly smooth and mutually enjoyable experience. Two of the plays, *Bang, Bang, Bang* and *This May Hurt a Bit*, have benefited from a workshop/research process. In the first we talked to human rights investigators working in the Congo, and for *This May Hurt a Bit* we talked to politicians, doctors, nurses, patients, hospital porters, bed managers, anaesthetists and phlebotomists working for the NHS. The play that followed was hailed as a trenchant, spirited and important defence of the NHS. I have always cherished your penchant for the surreal, and, in one scene, following an alarm, the arrival of the Grim Reaper, complete with scythe, on a hospital ward never failed to make me chuckle with delight.

There followed a shoal of plays voicing concerns about the NHS from writers as distinguished as Alan Bennett, Nina Raine, John Godber and Michael Wynne. Amongst this distinguished company *This May Hurt a Bit* scored highly, combining sharp satire, acute observation and political comment. Several critics hailed the return of agitprop, which puzzled you as you had never knowingly experienced that particular theatrical mode.

Bang, Bang, Bang was fun too. Franc Ashman, at that moment playing a Somali refugee, was tasked with smuggling her child from the Atlas Cafe at the corner of Thane Villas to Out of Joint's rehearsal room, a matter of 250 yards, which represented 250 miles. Various groups of actors playing pirates, warlords and UN roadblocks impeded her progress. The child was played by Clinton, a floppy life-sized child puppet of mixed heritage, whose first acting experience had been in Sue Townsend's *The Queen and I* and who was, by any standards, an Out of Joint veteran. Franc's distress as she tried unsuccessfully to bribe her way past a UN roadblock was observed by a concerned passer-by who had to be restrained from calling the police.

In another improvisation, in the alleyway outside the Out of Joint rehearsal room, one of our nine-year-old child actors, armed with a plastic AK47, was instructed to stop any passing 'car' (a couple of chairs slung together) and force the occupants to do anything she demanded. Gleefully she forced the other actors out of their 'car' and compelled them to dance like chickens. It was both hilarious and then rather chilling as she exploited her power and shot several 'chickens' who failed to please her. Chilling because it was exactly how a nine-year-old child soldier would behave. I recalled meeting a former child soldier, China Keitetsi, when researching *Talking to Terrorists*. China and her fellow child soldiers had ambushed an enemy camp at dawn and were instructed to 'kill every living thing'. Meeting child soldiers, Congolese warlords or cardiac surgeons is one of the unexpected privileges and pleasures that this work has afforded and I am delighted to have had the opportunity to share the experience with you.

I haven't met Sam Robards for some years, although we have occasionally spoken on the phone, but if he were to ask me the same rather peculiar question now I would now give a rather different answer. There is an upside to not touring and leaving home for 12 weeks of the year, and also to your not having to deliver or pick me up from work every day. Because, like any eight-year-old, I have to be dropped off and met at the school gates. I have not earned a penny over the past three years and you have become the very necessary breadwinner. Inevitably, when I was at Out of Joint our lives were shaped around my work, and now they have begun to flow around yours. That's a real upside too.

Already we have begun to see the fruits of this. You have been commissioned to write a pilot for a television series. You also have a commission from the Manhattan Theatre Club and an idea for a second TV series that you are starting to discuss. Your work remains original and witty, and to that you have added a political edge during your 17 years of living in our confused and fractured country. I am immensely proud of you and look forward to supporting and encouraging your work in any way I am able. I owe you that at the very least, for it is no exaggeration to say that you have given me back my life. Twice!

All my love,

Max

My parents met in April 1940; they married in June of that year; my father, Max Stewart, was killed in November and I was born the following March. It was a traumatic beginning.

My earliest memories were of men in uniform and I make no apology for including some of their stories. They are my ancestors.

There is a musical accompaniment to this letter. In about 1970 I was in New York directing *Dear Janet Rosenberg, Dear Mr Kooning* by Stanley Eveling, for the Hal Prince Organisation off Broadway. The hitch was I didn't have the requisite green card, so the company sent me to Toronto to have my passport authenticated by the American embassy. I opted to make the journey by rail, taking the Lehigh Valley's Maple Leaf to Buffalo and then on the tracks of the Toronto Hamilton and Buffalo Railroad to Toronto itself.

I love American trains and it was an exciting, albeit rather lonely, adventure. I arrived in Toronto at about 9am and completed my business at the embassy by about 10.15. After breakfast in a diner I had nothing to do but wait for the 9pm departure of the return Maple Leaf. I sat in a park for a bit and wandered through downtown Toronto. Arrested by some eerie music coming out of a record store, I went in and was told that it was a track called 'Song for Our Ancestors', by the Steve Miller Band. I returned to the shop twice more in the course of the day to get them to play the track again. For years I forgot about it, although my daughter, Kitty, and I became fans of other Steve Miller albums. She found it again recently for me, through the wonders of the internet. So now I would like you to stop reading and play the first three minutes of Steve Miller's 'Song for Our Ancestors'.

Dear Ancestors,

September 17, 2019

Like many people of my generation, my life was shaped and influenced by your stories of the Second World War. On my first trip to London the fat, elephantine barrage balloons were still tethered to the ground, revolving slowly in the wind. London was pocked with bomb sites which were gradually being turned into car parks.

My second father, David, was a Squadron Leader in Bomber Command. We lived in a rented house near the base, but when RAF Waterbeach was bombed for two weeks in succession by the Luftwaffe my parents moved to a semi-detached house in Bognor Regis on the south coast. (I remember the rusted scaffolding and barbed wire being removed from the beach after the war and a chunk of Hitler's Mulberry Harbour being washed up there.) It turned out not to be such a safe choice after all, as it transpired that Bognor Regis was a key strategic point in Hitler's invasion plans.

David's brother, my uncle John, was killed when a wing fell off his hastily assembled Liberator, which had been crated over from the USA. John's plane spiralled to the ground like a sycamore leaf. He was killed instantly. My father, David, kept John's watch on his desk, a burned and mangled icon. His name is on the memorial which leads to the Fellows Quad in Merton College, Oxford. He is buried in the pleasant graveyard of the Fleet Air Arm Church in Yeovilton, Somerset.

My father, Max, is buried in the rural setting of All Saints' Church, Buckland. Having won an MC at Dunkirk in May and achieved promotion on his return to England, he married my mother in June 1940. The Suffolk Regiment were then posted to Coastal Defence Duties in the expectation of a Nazi invasion. Max was delivering dispatches on his motorbike in the blackout when he crashed headfirst into a newly erected concrete block.

Max lay in a coma in a hospital in Frinton and my poor mother had a nightmare journey across East Anglia as the Home Guard had removed all signposts in order to foil the anticipated German invaders. Max never came out of his coma and he died on November 22, 1940. I was born four months later on March 17, 1941. His brother, my uncle Ian, was captured in Crete and spent three and a half years in prisoner-of-war camps in Austria. My godfather, Guthrie, was captured at the fall of Singapore, and he spent three and a half years in Japanese slave-labour camps, working on the Burma–Siam Railway.

This letter is written with all of you brave people in mind. It also incorporates your own words in excerpts from books, poems and letters you wrote.

After the war the family farm in Tring was tirelessly and meticulously managed by Max's youngest brother, Wren, until his death in 2014. After three years of Jarndycian legal shenanigans, the farm was sold and the estate divided between seven beneficiaries, of whom I was one. In a dank, windowless downstairs room that Wren had used to store sundry items of broken furniture, there was also a medium-sized safe. The beneficiaries were gathered as a locksmith finally opened the safe. The expectation of Spanish doubloons or a cache of white five-pound notes was disappointed. In the safe were Max's military cap and swagger stick, and about 250 handwritten letters. They turned out to be the passionate correspondence between Max, in France with the British Expeditionary Force, and Dorothy, my mother, a ward sister at the West Suffolk General Hospital in Bury St Edmunds. There were also dozens of theatrical programmes and writing journals. It seems that the father I never met loved the theatre and had a keen interest in writing. I only found this out at the age of 76. How curious to learn that I chose a career my father might have wanted for himself.

After Max's death my mother and I lived at the farm for the first two years of my life. We left when she married David, my second daddy, and somehow the correspondence remained at Lodge Farm. When I retrieved the letters they had lain unopened for over 70 years. Of course they were not written for publication. It is simply a record of two young people in love under the peculiar circumstances of war and possible imminent invasion. Max was 21 and Dorothy was 23. The letters from Max had to be passed by the military censor, so they contain no information about the progress of the war or his location. This information was supplied later by reference to a regimental history.

The Suffolk Regiment,
No 5 Company,
2EED
[British Expeditionary Force,
Just south of the Caen Canal]

May 18, 1940
My darling Dorothy,

You do know what your letters mean to me? Oh darling, sometimes I believe it would be too devilishly cruel if we were not allowed to be together and live quietly somewhere. God! What an adorable darling you are! I love you so desperately my own darling, darling Dorothy. This apparently interminable separation from you threatens to drive me crazy at times but it can't be much longer until we meet again. I will get leave soon, and of course it would be longer if there were to be a wedding! I feel so depressed when I think I won't see you again for months. Your photograph is my only consolation. What a lovely week you have given me. Every moment I was with you was perfect and I will never forget it no matter how many more wonderful times we have together. I have never been so happy. You are constantly in my thoughts.

Now the sun has gone and it is difficult to write more. The sky is pink, palely streaked through with blue and yellow.

Your beautiful photograph is on the tent pole. Your exquisite profile is illuminated by the candlelight. Goodnight.

All my love,
Your Max

Nurses' Home,
West Suffolk General Hospital,
Bury St Edmunds,
Suffolk

May 30, 1940

Darling, darling Max

I hope you are not too cold in your tent. I know just how wretched and lonely I am in a warm comfortable room but you – darlingest Max in your cold, cheerless tent – how utterly dejected you must be. I can't imagine anything more miserable than living in a tent miles from anywhere and in a strange country, but I'd be willing to put up with that if only I could be with you, my darling. I hate to think of you going to your little sleeping bag feeling cold and miserable.

I have to serve the dinners now and cope with my Germans. There are four German airmen in my ward at the moment. They are terribly polite and rather sweet actually. So pathetic and so so young. One of them proudly showed me the Iron Cross on his tunic.

How I love you – how madly I love you.

Your completely and utterly adoring Dorothy

The correspondence continued on Max's return, when he was posted to the Holding Battalion in Saxmundham.

By now Max and Dorothy were married and almost immediately Dorothy became pregnant. She writes to Max, 'If it's a boy he will be Robert Guthrie.' Those are indeed my middle names. 'And Catherine Jane if she's a girl.' (It's a coincidence, of course, that Kitty is a pet name for Catherine and Kitty is my beloved daughter.)

My uncle Ian was in the army, in the First Welch, and fought alongside the Sixth Australian Division in Crete. After the war he wrote a book, *The Struggle for Crete*, in which he records the bemusement of the British troops at the first sight of their Australian allies. The Australian Sixth Division had been plucked from the Western Desert and transported to Crete, where there was as yet no sign of battle at all. '*Germans appeared to have forgotten them,*' *To most of them it meant simply that they could get their boots off and lie in the sun or swim lazily among the rocks of the warm Mediterranean. Not greatly perturbed by the lack of those swimming drawers for which headquarters had made urgent application, they continued to flaunt their intransigence with a panache nobody else could match. The sight of a dozen Australians on tour in a stolen truck, their tunics open, cowboy hats on the backs of their heads, a rifle in one hand and a bottle of Krazzi in the other, provoked a certain jealousy. To the British, the Australians were a puzzle. Was it possible that they could be quite this wild and still fight under orders when the time came? The sober, efficient New Zealanders were easier to understand.*'

Ian Stewart's opinion both of the fighting spirit of the Australians and of their tactical acumen increased as the week-long battle progressed. One of the key points in his book is that the New Zealand commander-in-chief, General Freyberg, missed a vital opportunity by not ordering an immediate counter-attack on Maleme aerodrome in the first two days of the battle. At this point the First Welch, the New Zealand division and the Australians were fresh and had already demonstrated their fierce resolve, while the Germans had not yet exploited their air superiority and reinforced their initial paratroop invasion. However, as the battle continued, both numbers and equipment tilted heavily in favour of the Germans.

On May 24, General Freyberg realised that the only two alternatives were capture or withdrawal: he ordered a retreat and an evacuation. However, the fishing village of Sphakia, on the Cretan south coast, was the only port from which the Royal Navy could attempt an evacuation. The Allied forces had largely been engaged in the north of the island and evacuation involved a 38-mile trek across the mountains that formed the spine of the island, over roads in many places no better than mountain tracks.

Uncle Ian records:

Followed by the rearguard the men drew on towards the mountain aware of nothing but the need to keep going. Soon we began to climb. There was no talking. No man attempted to keep step with his fellow. Each plodded on. Like ghosts we plodded in the starlit gloom.

At the foot of the pass we suffered a cruel outrage. The engineers had brought down a fall of rock to block any German pursuit. Many hundred on the wrong side of the defile were forced to scramble on hands and knees on the face of the mountain. For the fittest it cost them nearly two hours. For many it called for an effort that was beyond them. And for the wounded it meant the end of hope. Hour after hour we trudged on.

Relief came at last. The night air grew sharp with the promise of mountain snow and pungent with the scent of thyme. As the sky lightened we could see that the road fell away through a narrow gorge and we could see no mountains lay beyond. Thankfully we moved through the defence line of the New Zealand Fourth Brigade into the unexpected haven of the Askifou Plain, a place of woods and fields, of birds singing in the dawn above tumbling streams, with all around the aromatic herbs and shrubs: myrtle and sage, rosemary and fennel. Smell is the most evocative of senses. Every man who was to reach there would carry with him the memory of this sudden quickening. For years he might forget, until suddenly without warning in some summer garden in Australia, New Zealand or England he would be reminded of this long-lost memory of his youth.

There was to be yet one more devastating blow. The Royal Navy had already suffered serious losses at the hands of the Luftwaffe, and their capacity to evacuate the whole army was insufficient. After the last ship had left Sphakia 6,500 men would be left. Ian was one of them. He was a prisoner of war for three years in Austria, firstly in a camp with Russians and New Zealanders, and for the latter two years with the Free French. He writes:

For me this time, which might have been the worst, became instead the best. More than all others these Frenchmen were able to live above their environment. For most of the time they lived and talked with easy wit and gaiety.

Ian was a skilled artist and I recall a series of vivid cartoons of his fellow prisoners that hung proudly in the living room at Lodge Farm after the war. He had also acquired a colloquial and very rude French vocabulary, which he paraded to hilarious effect when French-speaking guests were hosted at the farm.

My father Max's best friend at Berkhamsted School had been Guthrie Moir. After the British Expeditionary Force and coastal duties, the Suffolks were posted to Singapore and walked down the gangplank of the troopship more or less straight into captivity. Guthrie became a prisoner of the Japanese, working for three years on the Burma–Siam Railway.

Guthrie survived the war but struggled with the peace. In 1947 he edited a book called *Beyond Hatred* which gives accounts of various prisoners of war. He writes:

Return to freedom, when and if it comes, is weirdly compounded of ecstasy and disillusionment. The prisoner is in a unique laboratory situation in which he comes to realise he is both patient and physician.

Guthrie was my godfather and I remember him as eccentric and entertaining, but like many who had been through the war I think he had an unhappy and tormented old age. At his funeral his widow, Sheila, asked me to read a poem he had written about his own childhood, growing up in a Scottish manse. But in the same slim volume of verse I found this remarkable poem:

To Lieutenant Taramoto, Imperial Japanese Army

We did not mind your arrogance, your swords,
Your ape-like strutting progress between lines of soldiers.
We did not grudge your triumph, learned even to admire
Your passionate discounting of the odds.
I marked your moods as keenly as a lover
His mistress, or a psychiatrist his patient,
I had to, out of self-defence, and not
My own only, all the men as well whose fate
Hinged on your whim. They asked me pathetically,
How is he today? Is he talking of books, is he
Content or angry, do your best, they said,
To entertain him or it will be the worse for us,
And so the role of licensed jester racking
My brains for titbits, French, German, English,
To amuse. The novel was his hobby. Sometimes only –
That was when the sun shone early and work was easy,
Comparatively, and men died less freely daily.
Here now in Kerry, continents and decades away,
Am I feeble, I wonder, to ponder now these riddles?
It does not really matter, I studied you, my master,
Your every mood I knew, each twitch betraying
Anger or content, I did not exactly fear you

Even when you hit me, which you did often.
To me you were not exactly human, a force
Elemental, dedicated, incomprehensible.
And now your gimcrack bamboo empire's fallen
To dust. I ponder what you're doing. Dead,
Perhaps as you would have wished, on the job?
But other times, with the rains, the ropes like lead
The men were sick, sores, dysentery, malaria,
The work fell behind, eliciting inevitably your own joke,
'Best cure for dysentery is work, Mr Moir.'
For him it may have been but not for our living
Skeletons and scarecrows, perpetually incontinent
Retching, and relieving themselves endlessly on the edge
Of the jungle track we had hewn. They had no vision
To live or die by. Sometimes a torn photo
Of a wife they had barely known. They did not know
If they had children. They died without making a fuss.
And where is he? Is he dead as he would have wished
On the job in the jungle, on the pass by his railway,
Shovelled into a trench along with English or Indian
corpses? Or dead in a war criminal's grave
Scientifically arranged? Or is he still lecturing
In his beloved Kyoto University – on citizenship?
I do not know, nor care to know, only
I am glad I did not in the end betray him.
He was uniquely horrible, yet unique and complete
In his own view of war and imperial destiny.
Unique and untouchable, remote and incomprehensible,
I try still to understand you, Taramoto.

As Senior Medical Officer at RAF Waterbeach, my adoptive father, David, tended the hideous burns and wounds inflicted by flak and by enemy bombing, but he also became increasingly involved with questions of morale, and in particular the psychological impact of the extraordinary tensions endured by the bomber crews, with their constant proximity to death sustained over long periods of time. He played a vital role in the ongoing debate about 'Low Moral Fibre'. 'Low Moral Fibre' was never a medical diagnosis, but a punitive programme devised by a group of senior RAF commanders to shame young men into undertaking hazardous if not suicidal operational missions at a point early on in the war when losses in Bomber Command neared 50%. The chances of surviving a single tour of thirty operational missions without being killed, captured or sustaining serious injury was assessed at 44% and just under 20% of surviving two 'tours'. The air crew themselves, however, were even less optimistic and reckoned their chances of survival as somewhere between 5 and 10%. David considered the stigma imposed by LMF to be brutal and his report to the Air Ministry was important in influencing official RAF understanding of those who reported sick for reasons of psychological damage or nervous breakdown. In the *British Journal of Military History*, Edgar Jones, Professor in the History of Medicine and Psychiatry, concludes, 'Stafford-Clark's brother was killed flying in 1941 and his role as a medical officer during the war was a deeply held personal crusade'. The prolonged journey from LMF to the compassionate understanding of PTSD continues today in the armed forces, but David's pioneering work against stubborn and determined opposition is a cause of immense pride.

This work also led David to a lifelong post-war career as a psychiatrist. He wrote several books for medical students and for laymen, but ironically it is in a novel, *Soldier Without a Rifle*, that he most exactly reveals his bloody experience of war. A mistake in communication has led to two squadrons from two separate airfields exercising at night at the same height and at the same time. Inevitably this has caused a horrific collision involving the deaths of 14 airmen. I know this is based on a real incident because David told me so in detail. In this extract the Senior Medical Officer is searching for survivors:

We became aware of a terrible sound cutting though the turbulent roar of the now slowly subsiding flames: the shrieking screams of a human voice in torment. My flight sergeant was the first to find the source; one of the rear gunners. His body burned and torn almost in half below the waist, a few yards from his wrecked and partly melted turret. His pelvis was a charred mass of blackened tissue through which the bones protruded, both legs broken and dislocated at the hips, one whose baked flesh had split open down the length of the thigh. I had never seen a live human being more mutilated in my life. There was no hope of his survival. Flight Sergeant Gray handed me a satchel of Tubinic ampoules, little soft metal containers shaped like miniature toothpaste tubes with a sharp needle protected by a fitted plastic dome. Each held one-third of a grain of morphine – the minimum dose for self-administration in an emergency. I bent and straightened the elbow until I could make out the line of the vein. All the time the screaming continued. 'Right, steady his arm, please,' I said, and I pumped the contents of the six ampoules in rapid succession. The effect was almost instantaneous. The screaming ceased, to be replaced by rasping breathing which steadily grew quieter and easier.

I went to ascertain if there were other survivors. There were none. I returned after a couple of minutes. 'How is he, Flight?' I asked Sergeant Gray.

'I think he's gone, sir. I can't feel a pulse anymore and his breathing sort of ceased altogether.' He looked at me with careful regard. 'That was what you expected, sir?'

'Yes, Sergeant Gray – a peaceful, painless death among friends. Without a miracle that was the best I could do for him.'

Max and Uncle John were killed, but for Guthrie, Ian and for David the memory of their wartime experiences continued to haunt them in their old age.

David and Dorothy lived in Brighton, and I went down one day to take my mother shopping. I looked in on Daddy to pick up the car keys. He was reading at his desk and looked pensive. 'How are you?' I asked. 'I am rather sad today, Maxie,' he replied. 'I've been thinking of my brother John, your father, Max, and all those fine fellows I knew who were killed in the war.' These may have been the last words he ever spoke to me.

When I came back from shopping he was asleep, with his head on the desk. Gently I detached the book from under his arm. It was a road map of France and he had carefully traced a route from an aerodrome near Le Mans to a small port just south of La Rochelle. It was the route that he had taken at the fall of France. He was in Fighter Command at that point, and the Hurricane pilots had flown back to England in their single-seater Hurricanes, while the ground crews and medical staff had fled in an assorted convoy of ambulances, staff cars and petrol tankers. They got back to Wales in two colliers that had brought over coal for the French railways.

In *All Quiet on the Western Front*, Erich Maria Remarque writes:

After the war we shall waken again and then shall begin the disentanglement of life and death. The days, the weeks, the years spent at the front shall come back again and we shall march, with our dead comrades beside us, but against whom, against whom?

The ancestors in this letter had some of this confusion, but they also shared a firmly held belief that they were fighting to make possible a better world. David and Guthrie both voted Liberal in 1946 and Ian very probably voted for Churchill and the Conservatives, so I don't believe any of them were supporters of Attlee and the new Socialist vision.

But David's novel has an interesting passage: the speaker is a decorated veteran of the war who has led over 60 bombing missions and captained a Lancaster in the massive raid over Dresden. Speaking a dozen years after the war he candidly says that his biggest emotion was relief and surprise at the total absence of German air defences: "no flak, no searchlights, no fighter cover and no need for marker flares. Dresden was a carpet of flames that could be seen 100 miles away." He says:

I started out as a kind of idealist and I ended up, to my surprise, alive, with a weird mixture of relief, guilt, and an almost moral determination that we all shared a responsibility to create some kind of hopeful life and future for the world: something good, or at least better, to replace the evil we had been forced to confront in ourselves as well as in the Nazis.

Later – it must have been 1946, because David was still in the RAF but the war was over – we were staying at Lodge Farm and there had been great celebrations. Ian had returned from the POW camp and there was a huge bonfire in the Orchard Field to celebrate VJ Day.

Lodge Farm is two miles from RAF Halton and David might well have been doing some conversion course. Anyhow, he took me one afternoon to see the Lancasters and the big Stirlings parked randomly around the aerodrome, now unguarded, unregarded and redundant, waiting to be scrapped. He lifted me into the cavernous, gaping, empty bomb bay of a Lancaster, and I jumped down into his arms. It was a great game. After a bit we walked hand in hand around the grassy perimeter track to the officers' mess for tea. David slowly detached his hand from mine and wiped his cheek with the cuff of his smart blue uniform.

Casualty
March 1944 by David Stafford-Clark

'Easy, boys, leave it to the doc...'
'Afraid he's pretty bad, Doc, we've not heard
A word from him since just before we bombed...'
Hands under his arms and knees,
Lift him down gently; unplug his intercom,
And disconnect his oxygen.
Now guide his shoulders and dislodge his feet
From the wrecked turret;
So lay him down, and look at him.

'Much you can do?'
'No – I'm afraid he's dead,
Has been for hours—' 'Oh. Well. I'm sorry—'
'Yes,
Probably never knew what hit him.'
But in the torchlight you can see
His face is frozen:
Cannon shells pumped into his side
From neck to knee. Skin white like rigid lard,
Eyes glazed, with frosted lashes,
Flying suit crusted with red chalk
That was his blood...
Such is the cold
In a smashed turret open to the wind

Torn at that height and speed through icy darkness.
Yesterday
I heard someone complain,
'Last night the bombers in procession
Kept me awake...'

ACKNOWLEDGEMENTS

There are many whose help and advice were crucial in making this book happen.

Firstly, Stella, Kitty, my brother Nigel, and my sister-in-law Hilary. All were involved in this book from the beginning and their suggestions and practical help have been indispensable.

Secondly there is a group of friends who read the book at different stages of development. If you were to suggest that involving such an extensive group bespeaks a certain insecurity on the part of the author you wouldn't be far wrong. However, their varying applications of carrot and stick sustained me through the long months of lockdown. Their help was invaluable; Kate Ashfield, Gareth Armstrong, Danny Boyle, Dominic Cavendish, Caryl Churchill, Graham Cowley, Dominic Dromgoole, Dan Fredenburgh, Ramin Gray, David Hare, Lloyd Hutchinson, Roger Michel, David Rintoul, Ian Redford, Dinah Wood and Jane Wymark.

Thanks also to Jeremy Thompson and the excellent team at The Book Guild.

Dedication

Finally there is a wider group of friends and ex-colleagues, who in various ways have extended the hand of friendship over the last four years. I don't intend to imply that they condoned my behaviour; indeed most of them probably were uncertain of the details but in different ways they made it clear that they wished to remain friends and for that I am enormously grateful. This book is dedicated to them. April D'Angelis, Frances Barber, Richard Bean, Elizabeth and Frank Brenan, Patrick Brennan, Leila Bertrand, Howard Brenton, Rob and Vee Brookman, Sebastian Barry, D Bhatt, Lucy Briers, Alistair Beaton, Zoe Bedeaux, Michael Billington, Renee Bradshaw, Rachel Burton, Sherie Berk, Nica Burns, Ron Cook, Simon Callow, Simon Curtis, Allan Corduner, Panda Cox, Oliver Cotton, Chipo Chung, Dominic Cooke, Babou Ceesay, Jeananne Crowley. Lena Dunham, Adrian Dunbar, Alix Dunmore, Chris Dunham, Lita Doolin, Nicholas De Jongh, Jack Doolin, David Edgar, Ben Emmerson, Mehmet Ergen, Richard Eyre, Victoria Fairbrother, Nick Fletcher, Paul Freeman, Deborah Findlay, Hugh Fraser, David Fielder, Roy Foster, Stephanie Fayerman, Kathryn Grody, Peter Gill, James Graham, Andy Galloway, John Haynes, Elin Hansen, John Hollingworth, Carole Hayman, Lesley Huckstep, Nick Hern, Tim Hoare, Andy Herrity, Ken Houston, Robin Hooper, Elin Hansen, Peter Hartwell, Celia Imrie. Paul Jesson, Phil

Jackson, Des Kennedy, Mel Kenyon, Neil Kinnock, Holly Kendrick, Hanif Kureishi, Rebecca Lenkiewicz, Patti Love, Richard Llewellyn, Lesley Manville, Patrick Marber, Anne Mayer, Cassie Mayer, Pam Moiseiwitsch, Gregory Motton, Bill Muir, Bella Merlin, Ian McKellen, Blanche McIntyre, Sally McKenna, Pauline Melville, Marlane Meyer, Nick Marchand, Miceal Murphy, Anna Nygh, Leyla Nazri, Kathryn O Reilly, Thaddeus O'Sullivan, Mike and Meg Olmert, Ann Pennington, Olivia Poulet, Mandy Patinkin, Brian Protheroe, Pearce Quigley, Diana Quick, Claire Rafferty, JT Rogers, Ian Rickson, Sally Rogers, Tony Rohr, Paulette Randall, Wally Shawn, Robin Soans, Maggie Steed, Mia Soteriou, Jake Smith, Mossie Smith, Lesley Sharp, Danny Sapani, Trudie Styler, Denise Silvey, Karl Sydow, Jessica Swale, Trisha Thorns, Jack Tarlton, Gareth Thomas, Jo Town, Jenny Topper, Otto Tepasse, Manny Tsinas, June Watson, Jason Watkins, Tamsin Withers, Timberlake Wertenbaker, Karen Wookey, David Westhead, Jane Wymark, Harriet Walter, Danny Webb, Richard Wilson Angharad Wood, Graham Whybrow, Alex Yates, Ann McFerran.